MW00615167

Dear Readers,

This book is to my friends, my new friends, people who believe in me and Escobar Inc, my family, and in memory of my brother the great Pablo Emilio Escobar Gaviria.

This is my story, how it all began, the drugs, the money and the future of Escobar family, Escobar Inc and how we started selling smartphones.

Thank you God for giving me the opportunities throughout my life, for my beautiful children and for creating Medellin, the capital of the world.

Thank you Olof Gustafsson for your hard work and commitment, and your investments in me and my family, for working towards saving Pablo's legacy.

Thank you the people of Colombia, and the people of the world, for reading my book and I hope you all enjoyed it and learnt something about the life of me, Roberto De Jesus Escobar Gaviria, my family, and my brother Pablo Emilio Escobar Gaviria. To my mother, I love you. Roberto, your son.

Thank you to all clients of Escobar Inc and all people who believe in us!

Roberto de Jesús Escobar Gaviria
Alias « El Osito »

Alto de Las Palmas, Medellín, Colombia
January 2020

TABLE OF CONTENTS

THE DEAL

I walk to the control tower, and they tell me that the plane will land at one o'clock. I am wearing a pair of American shorts, untied leather sandals and a Polo brand T-shirt I had ordered from Miami. I was dying of thirst. I was sweating like a pig, maybe because of the intense heat, but also because of the anxiety due to the flight arrival. It was the first plane that would land that day. For my brother, Pablo, it was of the utmost importance. If things went the way that he had planned, his business would reach a major milestone. This was, our big deal about to happen.

The Peruvian drug paste was the most coveted in the market, and now he was a few minutes away from materializing a major deal. Pablo was waiting in the main hangar. It was built with wood and bright zinc, used for warding off the sun. The hangar ceiling was high enough to allow planes with a high tail, and also provided us with comfort away from the hot sun. My brother also looked anxious. However, his face didn't reveal any gesture of anguish or stress, but I was able to see through it, as I knew him better than anyone. He was anxious for the plane to arrive. He asked me how things were going, and I explained to him that things were OK, and that the last report looked completely normal, and the order we expected was coming in perfect condition. The rest of our guys were scattered along the runway, following the orders of José Fernando Posada Fierro, another one of our most trusted men. Next to Pablo, they had parked an orange-colored Nissan truck, which they had modified to have the cover removed in order to vent heat. The windscreen was removable to allow airflow, which kept the cabin cool.

Someone screamed from the tower that the plane was about to arrive. We all looked at the horizon, where we could barely make out an image of the plane. The intense sun created a hot, wavy light in the horizon, and the plane which was descending looked like it was melting as it lowered in altitude. Pablo saw the plane with a pair of binoculars and gave the order to our men to make the last minute preparations for the landing that would take place in a matter of seconds.

It was a powerful and wide turbo commander. It took off from an illegal runway in Peruvian territory, and at one o'clock it landed in the Hacienda Napoles. We waited a few seconds for the plane to taxi, and the beautiful plane was now very close to where Pablo was standing. Before the little door opened, I walked down towards the plane. I saw a person sitting in the first armchair. He stood up and took off the coat that he was wearing. He leaned his head out of the plane and he looked at everyone from the door with excitement. Pablo got closer to my side and he waited for him to walk down the stairs slowly and Pablo greeted him: "Welcome to Colombia, Mister Montesinos." Pablo shook his hand and with the other hand Pablo patted his back as a gesture of kindness. He was very courteous and excited, and he answered "Thank you for allowing me to come to your country and this beautiful estate." My brother Pablo answered him, "This is your house." This important Peruvian was wearing a long-sleeved shirt and a pair of beige pleated trousers. He used glasses with round little lenses, and a watch. He was perfectly clean and wore bright shoes. His smile was wide, and it unveiled his good taste in things as well as his greed. Pablo had told me about him. He said he was an important man in his country, since he knew the most powerful authorities in Peru. He had been an officer in the Peruvian army, in the rank of captain, and a lawyer, specializing in criminal law. You could easily tell that Montesinos had an entrepreneurial spirit. A combination of astuteness and intelligence, mixed with a hunger for power. Pablo, who had a natural ability to know all about a man before meeting them, had told me that besides his political aspirations in Peru, he was a powerbroker, a person who loved money and knew a lot of powerful people. Due to his connections he could become a great ally in Peru so Pablo was willing to please him with what were Montesinos greatest weaknesses: beautiful women and money. Pablo initially contacted him over the telephone, thanks to a pilot who worked with cocaine paste in Peru. By then, Vladimiro Montesinos was already an influential business man, a friend with great power, a professional lawyer, and a great trader. Montesinos was emerging as a strong and powerful force. Pablo made him get into the converted truck, and took him to the main house. We were in Napoles, my brother's most beloved estate, and maybe the biggest of all he had ordered to build. It was a limitless property. In the public documents it appeared with many internal venues, and without any fear of being wrong, I dare say that Napoles sheltered a large proportion of its sister departments, Caldas and Antioquia, or rather, its measurements began in the department of Caldas, and ended in the department of Antioquia. It had everything for those who loved the finer things in life. Houses with air conditioning, playrooms, swimming pools, bathtubs, jacuzzis, tennis courts, football courts, giant dining rooms, a theater, a disco, its own airport with hangars, rivers, lagoons, a zoo with animals brought in from Africa, streams to practice jet skiing, paddocks for horse rides, and a lot more. In addition, we lived in tranquility and safety, thanks to having the authorities of the area at our disposal. That was the place to be, a sort of earthly paradise built by my brother, Pablo, to which ex-captain Montesinos had just arrive to enjoy four days of drinks and rumba, but also to talk about important business.

That same afternoon my brother Pablo took him on a little tour around the estate. He showed him the lakes, the exotic animals, the pink dolphin, the roads hidden between the mountains. We made the route in the same orange-colored truck, as Montesinos had red cheeks from the heat. My brother had given him the typical hat that the illustrious guest immediately wore with both appreciation and excitement. Pablo took him to a village near the estate, called Puerto Triunfo, about 10 kilometers away.

There, in a cafe with seats on the street and under the hot sun of Magdalena Medio, we drank beer and brandy. Montesinos tried the brandy, but he preferred the local beer. We stayed there for an hour, and then we went back to Napoles. The truck parked for a moment while a worker opened the big door, in front of the main entrance of the estate, beside the highway, the same highway that links Bogota with Medellin.

Montesinos was impressed by the airplane that was hung above the main entrance. My brother explained to him it was a memento of his initial success in the drug trade. Pablo revealed to him that inside that plane, he had managed to bring from Panama about seventy million dollars, in several trips that turned out to be very risky for such a small bird. He told Montesinos that it was a completely useless plane that he had recovered and fixed. Once restored, its interior was fabricated with a reinforced floor, and they left only the pilot's chair. Inside the plane, there was enough room for bags full of money and for some extra gasoline gallons, which allowed for longer flight durations without the need for stopping. He also explained that because of it being single-engine, it wouldn't attract too much the attention to the customs agents. The customs authorities back then were very strict when it came to smuggling drugs over borders. Pablo emphasized to Montesinos that on top of the money bags, they always packed televisions and sound equipment in case the police discovered them. "It's better for them to believe that we're smuggling electronics instead of money," he told Montesinos. Montesinos was blown away by the story. Pablo told him that he had decided to leave the plane over the main entrance, as a symbol of freedom.

They immediately returned to the mansion. Montesinos was thirsty, and he needed to make some cellular telephone calls. During the return journey, they talked about politics, and about the special cases that Montesinos took on as a lawyer in his country. Pablo knew that his work in Peru consisted of leveraging his connections amongst the judicial and military authorities to get some drug dealers out of prison who were friends of his. It was clear to Pablo that great things in life were achieved when you have the right connections. Because of that, he never missed an opportunity to make friends with the who's who of Colombian and foreign politics. Later I will reveal further details about how Pablo managed to gain access to world leaders. Thanks to men like Montesinos, Pablo was introduced to world leaders in Asia, such as Fujimori, as well as leaders in Central America, in South America, and even in Europe.

That evening we were having dinner with Montesinos beside the swimming pool, and Pablo told me: "Brother, I also want to be the president of this country."

MY GRANDFATHER WAS A SMUGGLER

I was named after my grandfather Roberto Gaviría. He was considered the biggest liquor smuggler at the time. My mother remembers him as being nice and obliging in addition to being an intelligent business man. He used to be called "glass," because he vouched for everyone in town. He earned his money early in his life by chance.

One morning he was seeding some bananas in the backyard of the house and he discovered a buried treasure. It consisted of several little mud pots perfectly buried in the damp soil, and inside them my grandfather found jewelry. There were precious stones, earrings, rings, chains, everything made of gold. My grandfather and my mother used to live in Frontino, Antioquia. Every eight days he brought part of the treasure to Medellin in order to sell it in the public square. He camouflaged the little pots in corn and salt packages which farmers used to sell early in the morning. He raised money and he received a good reputation. He became a lender and charged interest to his borrowers, and the non-performing loans eventually made him go bankrupt. He didn't lose his sense for business. He liked hunting. He use to go to the place where the Native Indians from Choco sold fur, which he brought back to the village to resell. But since he loved making big money, he decided that his calling would be in something far more rewarding. From the Chocoan Indians he had learned the art of tobacco and liquor making. He travelled to where tobacco was wrapped and *Tapetusa* was distilled, which was a sort of prestigious brandy during that time.

After the Tapetusa was bottled, they brought it to the stores in Medellin. My grandfather knew that if he managed to move the liquor before the distributors could, he would have good profit margins. So he bought coffins from other villages' workshops. He rented a room with some people he brought with him from Frontino. He put the coffin in the center of the room, and then he made his buddies cry so that outsiders would think that it was an actual vigil for a dead person. Then they would go outside with the coffin over their shoulders, on their way to Frontino. Inside the coffin, instead of a dead person, there were packed bottles of *Tapetusa*, ready to be distributed. He also strengthened his business with tobacco imports from Panama. He was very smart. In Frontino, he built up a store in the same house where he lived with my mother. As he couldn't sell the *Tapetusa* in public, he used empty chicken eggs – that is to say, with nothing inside – and he filled the eggs with liquor using a syringe. His customers knew that when they asked for a "little egg," they were given an egg with the famous *Tapetusa* inside instead of a yolk. By that time, there were very strict customs officers, and this particular crime was penalized with prison time. Thus, my grandfather made his early fortune. But a woman named Clara Gaviría betrayed him. She told the customs officers where my grandfather bought the liquor from and that he also imported whisky from Uraba. The police came to the house, in which there was only my mother. She was very little, and the police enticed her with candy so that she would open the door. She guided them to the warehouse, and my grandfather was arrested for smuggling. I don't know how, but a few days after going to jail, another man showed up to get my grandfather, Roberto, out of jail. Another witness spoke in his favor and told the authorities that the real smuggler was a Cañasgordas man, who was also in Antioquia. The man was captured, and they let my grandfather out of jail.

MY MOTHER, THE TEACHER

My mother's vocation was teaching. When she was a little girl, she would teach the small children in her neighborhood how to pray. She became a teacher at a very young age. Her first job was in El Tablazo School. She started as a teacher and later became the director. She was really beautiful, she had big light eyes, thin and cheerful. Her brown hair matched with her skin color, and she dressed elegantly. On a Wednesday, a good looking young man knocked on the school door, and he caught her attention. He was riding a grey horse, and he introduced himself as the new administrator of the corner supermarket, El Tesoro (*The Treasure*), the biggest one of the area. My mother remembers very well that it was a Wednesday at seven o'clock at night. She opened the door thinking it was a mother who wanted to enroll a child. The handsome man, named Abel de Jesús, shook her hand. "No, I don't have children to matriculate, I just came to introduce myself," he said. From then on, twice a week he frequented her with evening serenades. He sent her greetings through the school girls. He gave her firewood for the school lunches, and he even wrote her lyrics of hit songs. He dedicated her songs with a loudspeaker and crank gramophone that he made sound himself. *Ojitos verdes* (*Little green eyes*), *El amor del jíbarito* (*The shuar's love*), *Yo tengo ya la casita* (*I already have the house*) became the songs which he played the most. By then, he was 32 years old and she was only 24. They became boyfriend and girlfriend a month and a half later, and within six months they decided to get married. She agreed, but she was transferred to a different school nearby in Campoalegre. One night during one of the visits, he left a pair of shoes sized 42 for her to store. She felt overwhelmed, and she told him she didn't want to get married anymore, but he convinced her about the eternity of their love. The only problem was his family. As a tradition, all relatives of Abel de Jesús got married with women of the same last name in order to preserve the lineage of the Escobars. So, getting married to a woman with Gaviría as her last name would tarnish the tradition. The priest of the town, Ismael de J. Muñoz, had to intercede. The priest convinced the Escobars that my mother came from a very good and distinguished family from Frontino, with a good social and economic standing.

They were married on March 4th, 1946, in Sufragio Church of Medellin. On January 13th, 1947, thirteen months later, I was born. I was the first one of seven children. Later, Gloria and Pablo. My brother was born on Thursday, December 2nd at twelve noon. By then, my parents had a home located in the village of Santa Sofia, in *La Cerámica* estate. Doctor Joaquín Vallejo Arbeláez and his wife were my brother's godfathers, on their request. They knew my father because he had sold them a piece of the estate. We all were born with a midwife. Pablo's midwife's name was Ramoncita. The first three of us were baptized in El Tablazo.

While my father was working, my mother was teaching in the village school. He used to take Pablo and I in the car, and he left us beside her desk while she taught classes to the girls of the first and second grade at the primary school.

My mother was later appointed director of the Titiribí School, in El Morro lane. At the time, Pablo was about two years old. My mother used to entertain him with singing, and she had school children sing children's songs to him. He tried to sing as well. He would sing a song composed by my mother, entitled *El Morrongo (The Beetle)*. My mother said that from when he was little, Pablo already had a good heart. He used to give part of his own lunch to the poorest children of the classroom.

We were all devoted to the *Divine Baby Jesus of Atocha*. The devotion began on the evening of the *Friday of Sorrows*, before Easter. By that time, everybody used to go to bed early for fear of the political related violence. The *chusmeros*, as the rebels of those days were called, had threatened my parents. That night we locked ourselves away in a hiding spot. At around seven o'clock, the *chusmeros* arrived. They threatened to make mincemeat of us with their machete. They said that they were going to take my mother, and that us children would be burnt along with everything and the house. My mother, started praying to a saint that was hanging from the little room wall, which was a gift from my father's mother: Sara Echeverry. It was Baby Jesus of Atocha himself, a saint indigenous to a remote homestead in Mexico. When the *chusmeros* brought down the gate of our house, the servicemen of the area showed up and they chased the rebels away. Since then, my mother promised that she would someday build a very big, beautiful chapel for the saint who had just saved all of us. Many years later, the promise would be fulfilled. The chapel was built in the neighborhood that would later be named after my brother, the Pablo Escobar Neighborhood, spending the money my mother had earned in bazaars, and from playing bingo. However, the church could not be inaugurated by order of a high leader of the time, claiming that it had been built with dirty money. Mom assured everybody that it was an act of hypocrisy, because my brother not only dealt with the priests using both money and cars, but also with several prelates of the country.

I think my family had always been catholic. My mother even told us that we were relatives of Father Marianito, the Colombian saint.

Because my mother's grandmother's name was Hortensia Essue de Jaramillo, native to Santa Rosa de Osos, an Antioquian village very close to Angostura, the place of birth of Father Marianito Eusse. According to mother, Pablo, myself, and our siblings all turned out to be first cousins of Marianito Eusse in the fourth or fifth generation.

Pablo and I began studying in primary school at a school called *Guayabito*, in Llanogrande. The school still exists in the same place today. Here we studied the first two years, and our first teacher was our mother. After that, we changed schools, and we started studying in the Julio Sanín School, in Rionegro. My mother stays in *El Guayabito*, and Pablo and I have to wake up at four o'clock in the morning in order to study by eight. Every day we went out on foot. We were very poor, and my mother would make huge effort to pay for our studies. My father did very little. We used to get out of school at four o'clock in the afternoon, and we returned home at eight o'clock at night. My mother packed enough food for us, because the daily walks were very long. We used to wear simple clothing, but they were always very clean. My mother used to tailor them so that we were always dressed up as well as possible. By that time people used to wear shorts, a checkered shirt, and a jacket over it. Sometimes we went to school with worn-out shoes. My mother was really ashamed whenever this happened. Pablo was once even sent back from school because of not wearing shoes. As her wages for teaching came from Medellin, the payments were constantly delayed. One day, my mother went to the public square and sneakily took a pair of shoes from the warehouse owner. She happily arrived at the house to give them to Pablo, but she discovered with great disappointment that she had taken one size 36 shoe and the other shoe was a size 35. In much grief, she went to the priest in order to confess what she had done. He forgave her. The priest understood the reasons of her sin, and he recommended her to go back and return them. So she went to return the shoes, ashamed. The owner of the shop gave the shoes to her, and he told her not to worry. She paid the shop owner for the shoes when she finally received her salary.

Another time, we needed to deworm our stomachs. Pablo had a huge belly, and a friend had advised our mother to give us a natural laxative. The friend gave the laxative to her as a gift, and we took the laxative one night before going to bed. The following day we both woke up with our entire bodies completely bloated, and our mother sent us to school. At school, we were the target of mockery, and we both cried. We rarely cried. I remember us crying only that one time at school and another time when our mother took us to the hairstylist because she shaved our heads except for a little bit in the front. "It's the current men's fashion," she comforted us. We also cried whenever they took pictures of us. We dreaded the photographer in his black coat that covered his entire body, who had us locked in a dark room. We thought he was the devil or something like that.

When Pablo entered third grade, and I entered the forth, my mother gave me my first bicycle. That was a memory that would remain with me for the rest of my life. The journey to school didn't take four hours anymore, now it was only 50 minutes, and Pablo rode on the special rack that the bike had. Going to study became a scenic tour. Despite it being a second hand bicycle that my mother paid in several cash payments, I took care of it as if it was new. Every day I cleaned it and I lubricated it, and a lot of times I avoided going to school because instead I rode behind the cyclists that trained through the road to Marinilla. I missed an entire year of school. So my mother and my father decided to move to Medellin.

Here, we finished primary school. Me, in the Gabriel Restrepo Moreno School, and Pablo, in La Mutis School. We came to live in the Villahermosa neighborhood. I studied the baccalaureate at night school, and then later I studied electronics. Pablo finished the baccalaureate in the University Lyceum. The professors complained a lot about him, because he was the leader of protest groups, and he made bold statements by demanding the heads of bad teachers, and he also protested for the replacement of other teachers. He finished studying that year, and he passed. My mother took out a loan to purchase the graduation suit for my brother. It was an *Apolo* brand jacket and tie, and a pair of lustrous shoes. However, Pablo was not able to graduate in public, because he was lacking half of a course. The suit couldn't be returned, and he gave it to a friend from the neighborhood known as *Rasputín*. When my mother found out about this, she was crying and she was very upset for she made huge sacrifices to buy this suit for Pablo, and she ended up hitting him. Pablo was a very good student, but he preferred to study on his own terms. My mother made him apply for the accounting program, in the *Universidad Autónoma* (*Autonomous University*). Pablo received the second spot in the program amongst thousands of applicants. The lack of money frustrated his aspirations. So, whenever he could, he bought law books, and he locked himself in the Public Library to read. He became self-taught, and he learned a bit about everything. He was passionate about Criminal Law. My mother still remembers that since he was little, Pablo had always told her he wanted to be a *Doctor of Law* with his own car.

One of his favorite hobbies was watching James Bond and Robin Hood movies. He collected them, and it wasn't strange to see him locked in his friends' homes playing them over and over again. My mother founded a school in the La Paz neighborhood, in Envigado, and we moved there. My father did very little when it came to domestic tasks at home.

By that time, I already began training to be a cyclist, and Pablo was my number one fan. He accompanied me to the local competitions, and he helped me to start my own my racing organization. I used to work in *Mora Hermanos* (*Mora Brothers*) enterprises, specialized in household appliances, because they saw me not only as a graduate and an electronics expert, but also a promising figure in both national and international cycling. The Mora Hermanos gave me my first sponsorship.

Pablo loved art and music. Even in the most difficult of times, in the middle of being chased, and of times when we had to escape from dangerous situations, he was heard singing out loud in the bathroom, famous songs like *Granada*, or *La Dona Inmovile*. He also sang Mexican mariachi songs. His favorite mariachi song was *Mataron a Lucio Vásquez* (*They killed Lucio Vázquez*), performed by Antonio Aguilar. His other favorite singers were Leonardo Favio, the Puma, and another one that was a Vallenato group. Years later, when he managed to amass his fortune, he would have the luxury of hiring to sing in person for him his most admired artists from around the world. Among many others, Pastor López, *Los Ayer* (*The Yesterday*), Nelson Henríquez, Los Visconty, los Chalchaleros, passed by Hacienda Napoles; he also programmed special events for people from the village close to the estate, with artists, and well-known comedians with national and international fame.

MARÍA VICTORIA HENAO, HIS GREAT LOVE

In the same neighborhood where we lived, he met the most important woman of his life. María Victoria Henao was studying in the *Liceo de la Paz* (*Lyceum of the Peace*), and she was barely in the fifth year when she fell in love with him. "I will get married the day I find a woman who doesn't call me to my home or doesn't keep behind me," he used to repeat to his friends. María Victoria never called him. She was pregnant when she hadn't finished school yet. Her first son was named Juan Pablo.

With a new obligation upon him, Pablo discovered an excellent way to work. He got Medellin insurance companies to auction crashed cars at a very low cost, and further declared as a total loss. He then fixed the cars and he made them as good as new in brass workshops that were owned by friends of his. He sold the cars to the highest bidders at an affordable price, but still yielding a good profit.

But he had another way of getting money. We had an uncle named Gustavo Gaviría, who had a marble workshop in Medellin. There they manufactured gravestones. Pablo used to buy the unfinished gravestones at a very low price. He then went around the Envigado parishes to find out if there were any people who recently died. He would go inside the homes where vigils were taking place in order to find out the names of the recently deceased. Once he obtained this information, he finished and painted the gravestones. Pablo made special designs with his brushes on the gravestones, which he then offered to the deceased's family, before their last departure to the graveyard. Pablo had an incredible sense for doing business, and a remarkable drive for making money.

HOW THE BUSINESS STARTED

Pablo definitely unintentionally followed in the footsteps of my grandfather Roberto. Having been involved in the business of buying and selling fixed-up cars, he met some important people in Medellin, who specialized in smuggling. There was a group of about 10 people. One of them who was known as *The Godfather*, another one whose last name was Bravo, Jorge González, and the best known was Gustavo Sanín, an important business man in Antioquia, who at the time was already amassing an incredible fortune with his yachts and ships, in addition to the offices and buildings in the center of the city. They made my brother a good offer that he couldn't refuse.

It consisted of going to the Antioquian Uraba ports, to coordinate the acceptance of boxes full of smuggled goods that arrived from Panama. They saw my brother as the perfect person for the job, because he had an incredible ability to convince people of anything, and they always seemed to believe him. That's how he achieved his first big success. He convinced the black longshoremen, who stole goods, not to steal anymore, and instead he offered them all jobs and incentives, such as raffles and gifts. At that time, the level of theft by the black longshoremen of the smuggled goods had the capos greatly worried. With no need to threaten the longshoremen, Pablo got rid of all of them. Because of this, the capos gained confidence in Pablo, and they immediately bestowed upon him more responsibilities. They gave him a car and money for him to lead a convoy of smuggling trucks on their way to Medellin. Once the trucks were prepared and filled with cigarettes, liquor, household appliances and clothes, Pablo ordered the departure. With cash in hand, his function was to pay the police that he encountered on his way so that they allowed him to continue on to Medellin.

This job lasted a long time. Pablo didn't smoke or drink liquor, and this helped him to inspire confidence from the capos. He learned so much and so quickly that the capos sent him to Panama. He used to come back in the smuggling ships to offload, and then deliver these goods to Medellin. He was delegated these responsibilities, and the capos even made him responsible for picking up the profits of the sales and to store the money in hidden places. Pablo had their full trust. One day he was called for an meeting with the capos. "Pablo, it's time for you to stop working as an employee and become our partner," he was notified. They explained to him that he would be designated as a partner without having to pay any money, and as a partner he would receive 15 percent of the profit.

Pablo had come up with a very safe system to store the money. He created special hiding spots in the walls of the houses, and covered them with polystyrene. He made electronic locks to be opened with switches, and no one other than him knew how to access the locks. The electronic controls, and the motors which moved the coves' doors were bought in a Medellin factory called *Puertas Universal*. Pablo's hiding spots were the preferred shelter for the money of the organization's bosses. Every two weeks, when they decided to make new purchases, the bosses indicated to Pablo that he should take the money out and bring it to a special site to exchange them for dollars.

The business became more and more successful. By that time, Pablo already had about 40 trucks under his control. Pablo was very popular in the little towns where his convoy passed through. His visit was always welcomed because, in addition to cash, he gave televisions away to the homesteads. He managed to allow all those villages to have black and white televisions. The trust he had gained from the police was eventually damaged, when a captain, to whom Pablo paid large amounts of money, decided to betray him. The captain was notified about his own transfer to a station in another city. The police captain took advantage of this particular situation when he received his typical payoff from Pablo. After the captain was paid, he informed his superiors about the transport convoy. He was likely expecting a raise or a promotion. All in all 37 trucks were captured, and at that time it was considered the largest blow ever that the smugglers had experienced to date.

Fortunately for Pablo, he was not captured, because the truck that he was travelling in broke down before arriving to the site of the police raid. He called his partners in Medellin, and they already knew about the captured cargo. He explained to his partners that he could speak with the high ranking officials for them to give the seized goods back. But they said "No," and they ordered him to go back to the city, but by the inter-municipal bus, because the car he owned had already been detected.

Pablo travelled by bus, and he passed by the place where he could see all of the cars and the drivers in detention. This happened near Palmitas town. He hired a lawyer, and after speaking with the judge, he managed to get the prisoners out of jail. The defense argument was invented by Pablo, who managed to get all the drivers in prison to agree to say before the judges that none of them knew the goods were illegal. Only one prisoner remained in jail. But a few months later, when news of the operation had already passed and the press no longer talked about the issue, my brother bribed the judge to let the remaining driver out of jail.

After this incident, Pablo retired from the business with a good amount of money saved from a few years of smuggling goods.

THE DRUGS

A man known as *Cucaracho* (*roach*), alerted Pablo about the existence of a better business than smuggling. He told him that it was not only profitable, but there was less risk because the cargo to be transported was much smaller. He told Pablo that the cargo was so small that it could be transported in a little car. They would have to travel to Peru. Pablo obtained his passport lawfully, and he travelled with *Cucaracho*, and he also took Cousin Gustavo, son of Uncle Gustavo Gaviría, the owner of the tombstones factory Pablo had worked with.

Cucaracho introduced him to his Peruvian friends, who explained to him how the new business would work. The idea was that Pablo and the other two Colombians would buy coca leaf in Peru and then transport the leaf to Medellin. My brother knew right away that it could be risky because in order to transport the cargo to Medellin, they would have to go through three different countries. The transport, as the Peruvians explained, had to be done by land, passing through Ecuador. Pablo invented a simple, but effective system. He bought a little car in in Peru, and he built a hiding spot inside the front mudguard. He also did the same modification with a car in Ecuador, and with another car in Medellin. Regarding the last car, I even remember the license plate: LK-7272. I remember it very well because that car was my personal property. He bought it for me without telling me why. I was dedicating myself to cycling, and I needed some extra money to build my first little house down in the San Javier neighborhood. I found it very difficult to get out of that little car because it was a fashionable car; a second-hand Renault 4 he had bought from Augusto Trujillo, then manager of Sofasa in Medellin, for only 55,000 pesos.

With the three cars, Pablo started making some trips. During the first trip, he returned with 1 kilo. After that, he raised the amount to 2 kilos. In a matter of months, he had already transported 20 kilos. Due to the fast boom of the business, the little Renault 4 could not cope. So he bought a tented truck with a larger loading capacity.

They had rented a house in the Belen neighborhood, and they brought all of the coca there. Then they converted the coca in rudimentary ovens, which crystallized the coca into paste. Once this step was accomplished, they packed it into double bottom suitcases, and they sent them with passengers on the way to the USA. The police didn't use sniffing dogs yet, and the Americans didn't have experience in anti-drug systems.

One kilo of this crystallized paste could go for over $60,000 in the USA. The shipment frequencies increased rapidly, and in turn the money was brought in from each load. The money was transported the same way that the drugs were.

Business went very well. My brother didn't want to travel to Peru anymore. They sent a driver to handle that, and the drug was packed into the spare tire of the truck. The truck went up to Ipiales, Ecuador, where they loaded up the truck with potatoes, in order to disguise the cargo at the border. One of the partners retired from the business. But before doing so, he reported the existence of one of the trucks. He did this with the purpose of letting some friends of his from the DAS[1] charge a percentage to the drug owners for allowing them to pass through. But one of the DAS agents, who already knew about the business, notified a superior. So, instead of asking for money, they decided to mount a special operation and capture everybody involved. The DAS agents let the truck pass through trouble-free until it arrived to Medellin. The truck was intercepted by DAS agents on the highway just before it entered the city. The detectives told the driver and his assistant that they should call the capos so that the agents could be properly paid, and if this happened the truck could then continue onward to Medellin. The agents explained to the driver that he should have the capos come with some money to a meeting at La Samaritana ice cream shop where they would finalize their arrangement. The driver called my brother Pablo and woke him up. Pablo called cousin Gustavo, and they both went down to the ice cream shop together. When they arrived, they noticed that the driver and his assistant weren't there anymore. My brother headed to the car, and he saw that there was no one inside. They went to the ice cream shop for the meeting with the DAS agents. When they arrived, they didn't see anyone, and they decided not to go in. They walked towards the corner of the street, and then they were immediately captured. They were taken to jail, and a summary was written about them. The driver and the assistant were already inside. They were taken to Itagui jail, and my brother

---

[1] Administrative Department of Security (in Spanish: Departamento Administrativo de Seguridad)

shortly thereafter was relocated to a special low-security jail in Yarumito, a special site for trustworthy prisoners, which had an opened door system. At that time, civilians were judged in military courts. One afternoon, when he saw an army truck arriving to pick up a prisoner, my brother felt frightened to be taken, and so he decided to run away. He jumped over the back wall, and ran. He called my mother, and told her what had just happened. He left a phone number where he could be located, and then he said goodbye. The jail director, who already knew both Pablo and my family, decided to also call my mother. He told her that my brother had just run away, and that it would be detrimental for him. He explained that if she talked to Pablo, she should tell him that the Army's intention was never to take him. My mother called Pablo immediately, and she took him back to jail herself. Pablo and I always did what our mother told us. That's why Pablo let them take him back to prison.

As the crime for which they had been captured started to be carried out in Ipiales, a judge from that city took over the case, and asked for them to all be relocated. Indeed, they were taken to Olaya Herrera airport in a military truck, and from there to Pasto by plane. There they remained a few months, after which they were let free due to the lack of evidence.

A month after getting out, they were captured again by the DAS in Medellin, but this time with the intention of killing them. They were taken to a desolate spot in the city, known as *El Basurero* (*The Landfill*), over the Medellin-Bogota highway. With their hands tied, they were taken out of the car, and at this point Pablo understood that they were going to be killed. My brother asked the DAS agents not to hurt them, and he told the agents that they were able to bring them enough money to retire, without the need to work for the rest of their lives. They unchained my cousin Gustavo, and told him to go and get the money. They asked for a million dollars. It was an amazing amount for that time. It was more than the biggest lottery prize. Pablo managed to make the detectives let him go too, as Gustavo came back with the money. Pablo and Gustavo then offered the agents more money if they let them know who had betrayed them. Both agents accepted, and confessed that it had been *Cucaracho*, their main partner. Pablo couldn't believe it. When they were unchaining them, he held the detective down and disarmed him. Pablo and Gustavo ran as fast as they could, and they bounced down the trash heaps in the landfill until they got away. Despite being shot at, they were not injured.

THE SOPHISTICATED DRUG TRANSPORTATION

This run-in with DAS agents didn't diminish his desire to continue in the drug business. Pablo, along with my cousin Gustavo, got their hands on a Piper Navajo plane, and they sent their plane to Peru. In this airplane, they would transport up to 200 kilos of drugs. Pablo discovered a new route to take more crystallized drug out of the country, and he did it using the same system that they had used for the truck. Within the spare wheels of the plane, they had packed the already refined drug, and then they sent the plane to Miami for repairs and maintenance. They labelled their merchandise with names like *Emerald* and *Diamond*. They used these code words when they talked about the merchandise with their American contacts, which made agents think that they were simply referring to precious stones. The tires filled with drugs were abandoned in the airport. Since the tires were in poor condition, the airport employees ordered the tires to be thrown into the local landfill. Then a garbage truck driver would naively take the tires to the main landfill, already outside of the airport perimeter, and there they remained. One of my brother's workers, known as *Bluyin*, discreetly tailed the garbage truck, and when Bluyin saw that the tires had been left abandoned in the landfill, he picked them up with a crane and took them to a secret location. As the drug price began to fall due to large supplies of cocaine already having been shipped to the States, the smuggling operation had to start running simultaneously in both New York and Miami airports in order to keep up with profit projections. The same plan was implemented twice a week.

My brother had such confidence in his plan that he gathered other well-known drug dealers of the time to offer them his transportation services, further assuring the delivery of the drug. That is to say, if the cocaine fell into the hands of the *gringo* agents, Pablo would repay the full price of the drug. In exchange, he would charge 35% of the value when the drug arrived at its destination. Pablo's fame began to extend among the drug dealers of Medellin. Many of them mortgaged their homes and estates in order to participate in the trade and they sent small amounts of drugs using Pablo Escobar's transportation services. Pablo didn't needed any more money to work, he practically made a living of other peoples' capital. The business flourished. The orders increased, and money came in huge loads. But another betrayal occurred. This time in the State of Florida. It was one of Pablo's workers, who revealed Pablo's masterfully planned system. However, my brother didn't lose any money because another partner of his found out that the *gringos* already had all of the information about Pablo's transport routes, and my brother Pablo suspended all shipments to the USA. "In every business, there's always a frog, especially when business is good," my brother used to say, and he always had a way of finding them. There were a lot of those so called *frogs* that my brother discovered. The business continued to thrive. He left aside the tire system, and he put another route into practice. This time, through Central America. He took advantage of a Jamaican route, and he sent his people to figure out a way to get the product there.

He bought an estate in Orinoqua region in an isolated part, deep in the interior where there's no population. In the back part of the house, he built an airstrip about 1,500 meters long. In order not be noticed by the Air Force planes, he built a homestead with wooden houses that had thatched roofs. He convinced families to live there, mostly hired people from Medellin. The foundations of the houses were on little wooden wheels. The homestead was located just along the strip. When the planes with the coca paste arrived from Peru, the town was notified over radio, and the workers moved the mobile houses on wheels, leaving the landing strip in plain sight for the pilots to make a safe landing. It was a very quick operation. Every family was obligated to move their homes in under three minutes. The same people took the paste out of the planes, and they loaded this paste onto a truck, which then went down to another site where it ran through the final process. Everything was planned by and ordered by my brother, Pablo. Pablo's creativity was unmatched. No one could ever surpass him. His orders had to be followed precisely like he had planned. Very close to that airstrip, hidden under the ground, there were cans with aviation fuel for the plane. The planes were refueled immediately, and went out again. In another location, my brother hid the already processed drug inside the rubber tanks, which were then covered with fiber and buried underground. He never allowed the paste, the aviation fuel and the drug to be all in the same place. Once the work had been completed, the landing strip was concealed again, and it was only opened when another plane was ready to take off to Jamaica with the finalized product.

The drug was packed in thick cloth bags, olive-green colored. Each plane kept its own flight plan. The idea was to have them all land in Jamaica in the middle of the night. On the landing strip, Jamaican workers received the drug in cars, which were parked on the edges of the runway. They took the drug to the ports, where they packed it in speedboats with fast motors, and they sent them on their way to the beaches of Miami. Sometimes the boats arrived at waterfront homes in southern Florida, which had their own private docks. The same system was used in the Bahamas, Jamaica, Haiti, and Santo Domingo in the Dominican Republic. But as the drug began to enter the USA in larger quantities, the authorities took greater interest in Pablo's enterprise. Pablo knew that agents in the USA were taking notice, and my brother decided to change his transport system. The airports didn't offer any guarantees, and the DEA began to fly over the Central American coasts more often. He created new routes that departed from Venezuela. The planes, with their new flight plans from Veneuela, went out to Santa Marta and La Guajira where they picked up the drug with the same landing strip system, and then they went on with their routes up to southern Florida. On each flight they took between 200 and 300 kilos. The new system was a type of bombing technique, which consisted of throwing the green bagged product out of the planes in mid-flight, but not on the Miami coast as it was done before. They threw them from low altitude into the sea, where fast motorboats arrived to pick them up, and take them to the beach during the late hours of the night. The system was later discovered by the DEA, but the DEA had a habit of figuring out how Pablo's systems worked around 3 to 5 years too late.

Pablo decided to change his transport plans again. He started to use legal routes for authorized goods, in which he disguised the drug. I remember the new system was put into practice with Chilean wine barrels. He used to send his people to Chile to buy the barrels. Before that would occur, the drug entered from Bolivia and into Chile through the frontier. Once in Chilean territory, the drug was mixed within the wine barrels. For this system, Pablo used the highest purity drug, so that he could prevent the cocaine particles from floating on the top of the wine. So, despite 10% of the drug being lost to the new process, the system was very effective. Apparently, the business was lawful. The system was used through each one of the South American countries, with the typical liquors of each region. Years later, this plan was discovered by the DEA. Again the DEA was late in figuring all of this out. The DEA invented the *narco-test*, a special substance which detected the presence of drug inside liquids coming through airports.

Later, Pablo used ships. For this purpose, he hired expert divers who placed the drug in the hull, in some special compartments that the ships had. Also on these ships, he took the drug out in PVC tubes, each with a 50 kilo capacity. The tubes had a special electric magnet that would attach to the underside of the hull. That's how it was transported to the coast of Miami, where one of Pablo's employees would wait with a radio-controlled transmitter, which they used to turn the magnets off. The tubes would then fall to the bottom of the sea, in a shallow part, and another diver would pick them up and attach the tubes to a smaller ship. I think the incredible power that Pablo Escobar achieved in the drug trafficking business was due in large part to his astuteness in creating systems to move drugs out of Colombia and across borders, undetected and in ever increasing amounts. For example, he was a pioneer of the narco-submarine. He came up with this idea in Cartagena, after the ships with drug cargos inside their bellies had been detected. He hired welders and shielding technicians, and he brought in all of the necessary items from different parts of the country, and other items he imported from Europe. He also hired engineering consultants from Russia and England to give him advice about how to build these subs. In Cupica, he rented unoccupied buildings in order to setup clandestine workshops near the beach. The submarines were not very large, and they were extremely useful and could carry between ten and twelve hundred kilos each. He had two subs built, and the journey took two to three weeks. When one of the subs was making its return voyage, the other one was being prepared and loaded with drugs. It was a safe and reliable system, which even today is still in use. The Russian engineers adjusted the remote control system. From its departure until its return, they were controlled electronically. Initially, the submarines arrived near beaches along Puerto Rico's coast. A tugboat pulled the drugs in closer to the shore, and the *frogmen* picked up the drugs and took them to fast motorboats. A major innovation was the anti-radar coating on the subs that the Russian engineers applied to the hull. This was one of the latest tactics that my brother used, even when he was still in La Catedral.

Simultaneously, he used DC-3 planes. These departed from Venezuela with a flight plan for New York. During the journey, the planes were redirected to an illegal landing strip in La Guajira, where they were loaded with two parachutes each filled with 500 kilos of coca. The operation was generally done at night. When the planes arrived in North American territory, the parachutes were dropped inside an estate of one of Pablo's American friends. The plane kept its route to comply with the original flight plan that was authorized from Venezuela. The plane would then arrive in New York with a lawful importation cargo.

Pablo soon discovered that the airdrop system was by far the safest and most profitable delivery system in place. The more planes he sent filled with drugs, the faster the money poured in. Loading a plane with a thousand kilos would yield an incredible amount of money, and it didn't matter to Pablo if one of his planes was intercepted. Thus, he decided that using many small planes with smaller loading capacities would mitigate risk and further increase profitability. He bought every plane that he could find that was in fair to reasonable condition, and he had the planes repaired. He eventually had a fleet of 15 aero-commander planes, each one with a 1,200 kilo capacity. They left in convoys during the night, and they arrived in the middle of the night to remote places in Mexico. In just one trip, he could move over 15,000 kilos. This meant $250 million dollars for Pablo with each trip. In 6 trips, he made $1.5 billion dollars. The same amount as an entire year's Colombian coffee harvest, which is produced by over 500,000 families.

Later, he bought older, yet still useful planes from reliable aviation companies. The expert in-house buyer for these purchases was my cousin, Gustavo. He negotiated with Eastern Air Lines for their Boeing 727 planes, before they had filed for bankruptcy. Each plane, without any chairs and without any other load, could hold up to 10,000 kilos of cocaine. The Eastern transaction was a clear demonstration of American double standards because they certainly had no problem taking Pablo's money for the purchase of the planes.

Ships were also regularly used by Pablo's organization. They were brought from Peru, with flags from different countries. He registered them as lawful fleets, especially fishing fleets, and he prepared them for loading the precious cargo. The ships were used to take drug paste out of Peru. Once in Colombian territory, they exchanged the paste for the already refined drug, and the vessel continued on with its trip to Mexico. The drug was disguised in fish flour bought in Ecuador. Each ship was able to move up to 15,000 kilos of coca.

Another small but very useful system, also designed by my brother, was the fridge system in the ships. Household appliances were bought in Colon, a free Panamanian port, where there was a winery. In Colon, electronics technicians modified the ships, and they created hidden storage spaces, covered with laminate. Each one could store 50 kilos. The secret was that large amounts of these ships transported lawful cargo loads. Also drugs mixed with tropical fruit pulp were sent from Ecuador and Panama in planes that departed from clandestine airstrips and flew to other clandestine airstrips in Guatemala. From there, the planes were re-packed and sent to the southern coast of Florida. A similar mixture method was used in Ecuador, but with cocoa butter.

My brother was the inventor of black coca. With help from the chemical engineers of the *organization*, the most pure cocaine was dissolved in special black paint, made from natural rubber. The mixture had to be made with a liquid chemical that was imported from Europe. Each 55 gallon drum could be filled with about 30 kilos of cocaine.

THE LAW

Monsignor Darío Castrillón was the last one to arrive. Pablo had him come from Pereira for him to be a spiritual advisor, and to take advantage of the closeness of the prelate to the current Colombian President, César Gaviría. My brother had told us in the living room that President Gaviría loved the priest very much, as he had performed his wedding ceremony. "That's the man we need, Gaviría pays attention to him," my brother Pablo said while looking at Gonzalo, Carlos, and myself, the only ones who were present in the living room of our friend's home in Poblado.

The Monsignor arrived about two o'clock in the afternoon. He greeted Pablo very warmly, he gave Pablo a blessing, and he felt happy to see Pablo in such a good mood. They were already good friends. In fact, Pablo was a very close friend of the church and of the priests. He dedicated a large part of his life to visiting the small parishes in Medellin and Antioquia, and he was frequently seen going up in helicopters once a month on the weekends to visit the most remote places in Choco or Uraba where he delivered gifts, dropped off supplies, and gave cash to the poor.

Pablo used to program special events with the priests during which he provided large sums of money, food and clothing. At Christmas time, he gave gifts to the children in greatest need.

"You know, brother, that my money is not mine, it belongs to whom needs it the most," Pablo used to repeat. Because of this, it made sense to us that Pablo would right now find himself having his picture taken with Monsignor Castrillón in the living room of this home in Poblado.

After the initial greeting, Pablo offered Monsignor something to drink, and then Pablo took the floor, and went on to explain the purpose of this last minute meeting. "Father, I want to turn myself into the police, but I need some minimal guarantees from the government," he explained to the priest.

Then he said, "The important thing is to finally end this war with the State that has claimed so many lives," and he explained that he was already working with a group of renowned lawyers and ex-judges in the drafting of a legal plan that would enable him and his workers' surrender to justice.

Monsignor was happy to hear what Pablo had just announced, and that he was willing to cooperate with the authorities. "That's what this is about, Monsignor," Pablo proceeded, "You are the person best suited for letting President Gaviría know about my plans, due to your closeness to him and his family."
Pablo explained that what he needed was for President Gaviría to know about his good intentions, and to give Pablo an answer as soon as possible. The priest accepted, and then my brother began to explain one of the plans that his lawyers had drafted, which allowed for his imminent surrender.

It consisted of several provisions that not only accepted his voluntary surrender, but also would allow for reduced criminal penalties for cooperating and confessing to his crimes.

Pablo had good attorneys. The maximum criminal penalty that he could receive was 30 years, minus a reduction in time due to the confession and voluntary surrender. He figured that a penalty of 20 years could later be reduced to about seven years.

Monsignor listened attentively, and in the afternoon he went through a list of advantages that this surrender would give to both Pablo and to the country. For Pablo, it was clear that his surrender would bring tranquility, not only to the country, but also mainly to our family; to my mother and my sisters, and of course to all of our children. Things rapidly intensified. Firstly, because of the Nation's persecution of him and our family, and secondly, because of the war with the Cali cartel. From jail, Pablo would be able to fix problems more effectively, and we would gain the added bonus of being closer to our families.

Because of this, he had already planned out and prepared the land where he wanted to build his own jail. "The only thing left is for the government to agree to these terms," he told everyone.

The meeting ended at eight o'clock in the evening, amid great optimism and with the hope of receiving a prompt reply from the President. Three months later, and the effects of that that meeting formed a part of Colombian history.

The estate where Pablo spent the last days before his surrender was called *Perrito Flaco* (*Skinny Dog*). He had called it that because when he bought it, the property came with a scrawny looking mutt. It was a really lovely estate, and there was a small ravine around the house. The location was really special, in the hills of Envigado, surrounded by trees and with an amazing view. We arrived just three days before the surrender. I think it was June 19th, 1991. We were there with Pablo, our mother, our wives and our children. There was also a very renowned doctor from Antioquia, who was with Pablo during the months leading up to the surrender. He handled things for Pablo. He brought the mail back and forth to the post office, and he was the liaison between Pablo and his lawyers who were negotiating and planning the surrender.

My brother had bought the estate five months ago, and he used it as a hiding place to prepare for the surrender.

That day, Pablo woke up much earlier than he typically would. He used to sleep until ten or eleven in the morning. That morning he woke up early at around seven, and he got ready. My mother and Pablo's wife prepared breakfast. At nine o'clock we began arranging for a helicopter that would take my brother to the *La Catedral (The Cathedral)*. The helicopter belonged to the government in Antioquia. A big yellow-colored Bell helicopter, which was used by the governor to travel around the department. The helicopter left from a government building, on its way to a football arena in the hills of Envigado. After midday, we started to get the cars ready, two Renault 21s. Later Otto and Popeye arrived to escort Pablo to La Catedral. I personally drove my brother in one of the cars. We took two 25kHz Motorola radios that operated on two different bands. Pablo had dressed himself up as always in a pair of American blue jeans, Adidas trainers with white studs, and an Italian T-shirt with buttons. He took nothing else. Not even his silver chains. Just a Cartier watch with a leather band, and a Sig Sauer hand gun that he always carried. The drive up to the arena lasted eight minutes. The helicopter arrived on time, and it took only a few minutes for Pablo to go inside. There was a Medellin reporter at La Catedral, and other people that I don't remember. Before going in, he gave me a hug, and then he gave me the number to a mobile telephone that he carried. "Call me when you know I have arrived," he told me. It was a telephone from Medellin Public Enterprises. I still remember the phone number: 3480185. It was a phone that he used for his family, which came in a little briefcase with a battery and everything.

Fifteen minutes later, he called me from La Catedral, and he told me everything had gone OK. "Don't worry, I am organizing everything to allow everybody else to surrender too," he told me.

I went back to the house where he had originally been in hiding. In front of the fourth brigade, in a two-floored apartment. I spent the whole day there, training in the morning; on a stationary bike and on a treadmill. At night, I used to go out by car to the center of the city, and sometimes I would go to ice cream shops in Junin. I wore a wig, dark glasses, and I let my beard grow. After Pablo's surrender, we talked everyday over the phone about everybody's planned surrender, including my own. I really didn't want to go before the courts, because I didn't have an order to be captured or any problems with the law. I really didn't see the need for my surrender. What happened was that my brother had received information that said they were looking to kill me. "Surrender quickly, brother, you will be safe here, nothing will happen to you in La Catedral, we will solve everything when things calm down," he warned me.

Then I finally made the decision to surrender. I went to my mother's house to eat and to also tell her that I was finally going to do it. I was going to surrender. She was scared when she saw me. I explained to her that I had to surrender because Pablo indicated to me that my life was in danger if I was to remain all alone without any protection. I also insisted that it was best for her to come up to La Catedral and visit us from time to time, and she could keep living in her house. She understood my reasons for the surrender. We ate dinner together. We prayed together and recited the Holy Rosary. I asked for my mother's blessing, and I left her house and travelled back to my hiding place.

The following day, I took a taxi up to Envigado Park because that is where we had planned for me to be picked up. I entered an ice cream shop named *El Paraíso (The Paradise)*, I drank two glasses of red wine, and I waited about an hour. I left the shop, and I walked through the park on foot. I knocked on the mayor's door, and he got scared when he saw me, and then I explained to him that I was going to surrender. I called Doctor Martha Luz Hurtado by phone, and she picked me up from there. She was the director of criminal procedures of Antioqua, and she was also the one in charge of preparing the surrender of my brother's men.

Doctor Hurtado arrived in an official car, and we left on our way to La Catedral. She explained to me that in La Catedral there was a judicial officer waiting for me to take my declaration and a doctor to give me a medical exam.
We went up the mountain about six kilometers through an uncovered steep road with cliffs on both sides. It was about a 25 minute ride until we had reached the main entrance to the jail.

My brother Pablo received me, he hugged me and he told me not to worry, that I would be OK. "Sit down and have some coffee." He took me by the arm and led me to the dining room. I was wearing a pair of beige linen trousers, a blue shirt, sport shoes, and I carried 50,000 pesos cash.

I asked Pablo if he had already spoken to the officers regarding permission for family visits. He explained that he had, and later the judicial officer arrived to take my first declaration.

He told me that the requirement for the surrender was for me to confess a crime. I started thinking about which crime I would choose, and a few seconds later I told her: Well, doctor, I'm going to confess the Rh crime. Everyone looked at each other astonished, Pablo laughed and the doctor told me that crime wasn't in the code. *"What do you mean by that?"* she scolded me. I told her, "No, doctor, the Rh crime is to have the same blood type as my brother Pablo, 'O' positive." This was my first declaration.

At 12:30, we had wine marinated chicken for lunch, and I kept making declarations that afternoon. I was arrested, and brought to justice for the crime of illicit enrichment.

I stayed in the hall, chatting with Pablo, some people from the government, and several of the guards. I talked for a while with my two friends, who escorted me to my official surrender. They were Vinicio Echeverry Arango, a 74 year old doctor with whom I used to ride with, as well as the cyclist, Ramón Hoyos Vallejo. We reminisced about sports and cycling. I was really calm because I had never before imagined the day that the legal torment and persecution would begin. The afternoon rapidly passed by, and I went to sleep at eight o'clock in the evening, I was really tired. I got up at nine o' clock in the morning with the idea of taking a tour all around the jail, and I especially wanted to find a trail to take for my daily jog. That day, I was able to exercise because Pablo's men had already started to build a gym with some equipment they had brought to the jail. I jogged, I walked, and I did push-ups at around twelve noon. We ate meat and potatoes for lunch with Pablo. That was one of my brother's favorite dishes. He ate well, and in true Medellinean style. At night, for example, his favorite dish was rice with eggs, accompanied with fried ripe bananas. People have the impression that Pablo Escobar was a really big, fat guy. Before being in La Catedral, he never weighed more than 78 kilos, which was actually his average weight. He was about 1.68 meters tall. He may have looked fat because of his neck, where he had a double-chin, and he also had a little bit of a belly. He had small hips, and he used keep taking his pants up with his hands. Almost always, he wore a pair of American blue jeans, except for when he was engaged in politics.

Midday on July 22nd, we talked about making some improvements to the jail, and we also talked about some other ideas that were running through Pablo's head. He talked about the need for building an air-raid shelter, because he was obsessed with the idea that his enemies from Cali wanted to kill him in a bombing run from one of their planes. He explained all of the reasons as to why he chose that particular plot for the jail site. Pablo had seen two other sites in Antioquia. "This is the place, brother. Did you notice yesterday that after six o' clock in the evening it gets full of fog, and at dawn it's covered as well?" he told me in the dining room. I agreed, and I asked if he had already thought about where we would build the shelters, and he took me to the west side of the building and then pointed to a higher position in the jail, behind the last wire fence, where the tallest trees grow. Pablo had been very clever. La Catedral jail was built with Pablo's money. Who else would be responsible for the official cost of its construction? In the negotiations for his surrender to Cesar Gaviria's government, my brother made it very clear that no tree in that area could ever be cut down for any reason.

That afternoon he reminded me of how important that little detail was. "From above," he insisted, "they will find it very difficult to target us."

He was right. He showed me drawings and photographs of the entire place. He formulated the plans for the jail long before his surrender. La Catedral was located at the steepest part of the mountain, about 7,000 feet above sea level. It didn't have easy access, and it was surrounded by smaller mountains. La Catedral had the most incredible views. You could see Medellin in all of its magnificence, from the Medellin train routes to the stadium and a little Medellinean village. From there, you could catch a glimpse of the three main access routes to Itagui and Envigado, and almost the entire main road leading up to La Catedral. The road looked more like a gray snake seen from the little balcony in which Pablo and I looked down from together.

Altogether, the field of vision covered an area of about 30,000 square meters. The name of my brother never appeared in any of the documents, of course. But it was Pablo himself who picked up the land, using straw buyers. All this was always kept a secret from the government. An Envigado ironworker purchased the land in 1990. The same old man, an acquaintance of the family, exchanged it with the municipality, in a totally legal transaction that was even registered with a Medellin notary in 1991, if my memory serves me correctly. The ironworker, was an old man who had purchased the land from a woman, also a friend of ours, who had received another much smaller parcel in exchange. The site had everything, and was already hooked into the electrical grid. It just needed some fixing up. La Catedral looked like a school in a small village, surrounded by a wire fence.

Despite the site being found in uninhabitable conditions, Pablo and I always thought that, according to the agreements with the Government, we had every right to make some changes to the structure. The jail was named La Catedral, because that was the name of the mountain where we built it.

Half-jokingly, and while we looked at the beautiful valley down below, I told Pablo that we should install a telescope so that we can watch the Medellín and El National football matches, and we both laughed. Medellín was his beloved team, although he also showed some devotion to El Nacional and, of course, our home team, the Envigado. Later, I will talk more about my brother's obsession with football. A sport that he never stopped playing, not even in jail. He brought the three best teams in Medellin to play at La Catedral. He paid them well. The clubs and their coaches loved Pablo's money.

"I will order a telescope very soon, but not to watch the football matches. Rather, I would like to have a complete visual of everything that's going on down there."

He added that football matches could be seen from a giant screen, or in La Catedral itself. "A live broadcast of ourselves playing," he emphasized.

That's how we spent a large part of that first day in La Catedral. We then focused our attention on the men who were soon to arrive in the jail, as his most trusted workers were now complying with their own surrender. Pablo wanted all of them to stay in La Catedral where they would be safe. He even discussed his ideas about different legal routes that would allow his men to more easily surrender.

Now I remember a situation where 3 of his men did not have any crimes to confess. Pablo gathered them together, and told them to come up a fake story about a drug delivery in which the three of them had participated. They agreed, and concocted a story about a 400 kilo drug deal. "When you confess, say that you borrowed a blue-colored Chevrolet dump truck. Say that you drove it, and then say that you loaded drugs into the vehicle," Pablo explained to the guys. He warned them not to forget about the car's color, and to always say that Pablo owned the merchandise. So they agreed, and so it was done. Except that in a third inquest, the three of them gave a different color for the car. That's exactly how one of the invented crimes was confessed. I think one of these guys is still in jail.

In the days to follow, Luis Carlos Aguilar Gallego aka *El Mugre* (*The Dirt Guy*), Otoniel Jesús González aka *Otto,* Valentín Jesús Taborda, Gustavo González Flórez, Juan Enrique Urquijo Gaviria (Our Cousin), Jorge Eduardo Avendaño Arango aka *Tato*, John Edison Rivera Acosta aka *El Palomo* (*The Dove*), José Fernando Ospina Montoya aka *El Gordo* (*The Fat Guy*), John Jairo Betancur Montoya aka *Icopor*, Luis Carlos Diez Bedoya aka *La Garra* (*The Talon*), Alfonso León Puerta Muñoz aka *El Angelito* (*The Little Angel*), and Luis Fernando Henao Giraldo aka *Misil* (*Missile*), would surrender. Pablo would always receive them personally at La Catedral. These men hadn't seen my brother for a long time, and they always had a lot of catching up to do. They also brought a good number of magazines about my favorite sport, cycling. French, Italian, and some Colombian magazines were also brought in. As for Pablo, his obsession was football, and as for me it was cycling. Since my youth,

I've been hooked on the sport. I became a cyclist in 1962. At 15 years old, I already belonged to several municipal clubs. I even got to ride alongside cycling stars such as *Cochise* Rodríguez, *El Ñato* Sánchez (*The Snub Nosed*), and Buitraguito. As a professional, I received a sponsorship from Mora Hermanos, an enterprise for which I worked as an electronics technician. With that sponsorship, I ran my first Vuelta a Colombia, in which I came in 19th place. I represented Colombia in the Vuelta al Táchira in Venezuela, in which I came in fourth place in La General. In 1966 I went to the Juegos Bolivarianos y Panamericanos, and I won the gold medal in a 100 kilometer race against the clock, being on a team with Alvaro Pachón, *Cochise* and Severo Hernández. I held a new record for the most wins with 37 stages in the same year. Soon after I retired, I become Antioquia's coach. My team beat the best teams in the world. Later, I was named coach of the official Colombian National team. We won the Vuelta a Cuba, La Vuelta al Táchira, the *Gran Premio Jalisco* in Mexico (*Big Jalisco Prize*), and the Vuelta a Costa Rica. I retired from coaching, and I built a bicycle factory in Manizales named *El Osito (The Little Bear)*. During many of the competitions, my brother Pablo was beside me. I even keep pictures from when Pablo, who was just 13 years old, appeared to support me while I raced.

It was from my days as a cyclist where I got the nickname *El Osito*. It was during a stage in which I had been the first to arrive at the checkpoint line for Medellin, and right after I crossed the line I fell into the mud. I lost a lot of time. I recovered, and I left behind Cochise and Ñato Suárez. When I passed by the race leaders, who were Pastor Londoño y Carlos Arturo Rueda C., they couldn't recognize me because I had mud covering everything, even my nose, and they said, "Here comes a guy that looks like a little bear!" The nickname has stuck with me ever since that day.

I was even a sports reporter and a special correspondent as a photographer during the World Cup that took place in Bonn, Germany. There I met the well-known journalist Héctor Urrego, whom I helped to operate a small camera that was called the *110*. Héctor hadn't taken a photographer with him, and so I served as a graphic reporter among Japanese, German, and American photographers that seemed to humiliate me with their powerful and large lenses which were hanging from their backs. Whatever the case, I took exclusive pictures of that World Cup. I accredited myself as part of the international press, and I once helped Héctor Urrego to enter a stadium because he didn't have a card or the credentials as a photographer. I completely retired from cycling when the authorities started going after my brother, Pablo.

LIFE IN LA CATEDRAL PRISON

That's how my first few hours in La Catedral passed by; reminiscing and reading. Besides cycling magazines, I had brought with me a book entitled *Cómo Obtener Una Supermemoria* (*How To Have A Super-Memory*). A special friend, who knew about my surrender, gave it to me as a gift.

The first visitor that we had was my mother. The first Sunday she arrived, as always, accompanied by a rosary and a cold meat pot that she prepared at home. The cold meat she brought was very famous in Medellin, it's a sort of tamale. She cooks the chicken, meat, rice, potatoes, and yucca, and then she wraps this it in a thick banana leaf, she ties it with a sisal, and then she serves it. That's what she brought for her first visit. She also brought pictures of saints and the Virgin in order to decorate the little chapel, which my brother ordered to be built. Pablo, as I said before, was very religious. Three days after having arrived, he confessed his sins, and he made every single one of us who had just arrived, also confess. He and I confessed to Father García Herreros, a little priest who was really loved by our family, and whom my brother considered a living saint. We confessed all of our sins that day. We all have sins. We asked God to help us get out of this situation in which we were currently stuck, especially because our family was being persecuted.

Pablo had seen the Father on television, on a show that he had every night at seven, before the newscast. The priest's show was called *El Minuto de Dios* (*God's minute*), and Pablo knew that everybody used to watch the show, and he really believed the messages that Father would give. That's why he contacted him, almost one year before his surrender. I believe Father García Herreros had a lot to do with my brother's decision to surrender. They met often, and Pablo had helped him with his campaigns to help homeless people and for his church in the Minuto de Dios neighborhood in Bogota. The Father listened to Pablo, and advised him often, and through the television program, he sent coded greetings for Pablo along with spiritual guidelines. It was important for the oversight of the surrender process. Some of the encrypted messages from the priest during Minuto de Dios were actually revealing details about the locations where they had finalized his men's surrender. Once in jail, the father visited us with a certain frequency. For Pablo's first confession, he brought a big white ruana blanket from Bogotá, made of pure sheep's wool that helped Pablo to keep himself warm during those cold the nights at La Catedral.

Father was there on the first Sunday in La Catedral, and it was he who performed the first mass for the prisoners. Everybody invited their relatives, and after the mass we devoted our time to our children. Pablo had ordered a special playground built for them, with a dollhouse for the girls in the part below the corridor where our rooms were. When night came, everyone left. My brother and I talked in the corridor about the agenda for the week ahead.

As the idea was for us to keep in good physical condition, we decided to build a football court. Currently, there was only half of a court, and it was very small. What we did next was modify the court to professional arena specifications. We extended the court, and we fixed everything ourselves. There was a constant flow of visitors that came to La Catedral, and people always came to watch our football matches. The matches that were played in that stadium will go down in history as being some of the most hard-fought, difficult, and prolonged matches in professional football. For almost the entire day we worked in that arena, and it took weeks for us to have everything organized properly. We ordered the goals and nets from a workshop in Envigado, and instead of grass we used dirt from Amaga, Antioquia.

THE BIG SPORTS TEAM IN LA CATEDRAL PRISON

Months later, Pablo would fulfill his promise. He made the most of *Las Mercedes* celebration week, which in Colombia is the saint of the prisoners. Soon thereafter he invited to La Catedral the three main professional football teams in Antioquia: Atlético Nacional, Medellín, and Envigado. He was fanatic about Medellín. As for myself, I was a fan of El Nacional. The first team to play in the jail was El Nacional, with all their star players that were already internationally renowned and famous. I remember about the spectacular goalkeeper René Higuita. My brother called him *El Loco* (*The Crazy Guy*). Pablo had met him when he visited the most deprived areas of Medellin to give money to the small schools, and to build well-lit football courts, basketball courts, swimming pools, and running tracks. He also used to bring uniforms and professional footballs to the local teams. He met Higuita in the Castilla neighborhood. He was a really humble guy. Within that area of Medellin, there were a lot of players who had just started. It captivated my brother from the first moment, and Pablo discovered the talent of a great goalkeeper within it. My brother helped him with his early career as a footballer, thanks to knowing the owners of several professional clubs. René is, up to this day, one of the most internationally renowned goalkeepers, and one of my best friends. I still think he was put in jail unjustly; solely because he was a friend of Pablo and myself. The judge did not believe that he had helped to free a kidnaped little girl, and they instead accused him of being involved with her kidnapping. It was all completely unjust. But time proved him right.

Leonel Alvárez, another good friend of ours, also participated on the team. Leonel and René would visit us later, during a special scenario that I will recall later. Another one I recall with great affection is Faustino Asprilla, the Colombian player, who played the game brilliantly. Of course, there was the very beloved Andrés Escobar, who would later die in the craziest way in Medellin. There was JJ Tréllez, Barrabás Gómez, *El Chontico* Herrera. Every team in those days needed to have at least half of their roster consisting of Colombian nationals. The idea was to play against them within all the playing rules. "Well, guys, the matches last three or four hours here, without any type of break," my brother shouted from within the arena. El Nacional used its official uniform, and we used ours, which was the same uniform as the German national team. Pablo then gave more instructions: "There are only two player changes allowed, and if there's a tie, the match will be decided with penalties," he explained to everyone. My brother wore number 9 on his uniform. A young man, who was one of the prison guards, played too. I was in the midfield. Also on our team was *Popeye*, *Angelito*, *Misil* and *Mugre*. There were family visitors watching us play. In the first 50 minutes El Nacional scored three goals. An hour and a half later, the match was already tied. Tellez scored the fourth and Leonel the fifth. When there was half an hour left, we tied the match. My brother made a huge goal from outside the 18 yard box. He was good at kicking the ball from far away. He was really dangerous with his left foot. Pablo was followed by Leonel. During the entire match, he put pressure on Pablo, and he didn't let him pick up the ball. Leonel grabbed his T-shirt, he made him trip, he grabbed his hair, he put his nails on him. Pablo complained and Leonel said "This is how we really play football, brother." The match ended 5-5, and went to penalties. I think that's where René helped us, because he missed a penalty and he let my brother score a goal, which was powerfully sent to the center of the net. "No one will be able to block this," my brother said to him before going in for the kick. We won thanks to penalties, and we beat the powerful Atlético Nacional. After that, the pictures with our children, our relatives, and with the players, who were their idols, would take place. Everybody wanted their picture taken with *El Loco* René.

Days later we received the Medellín and then Envigado visited. Both teams played with their official uniforms. We never lost a match. From those matches, I remember the Envigado coach very well, the famous *Chiqui* García. He was one of the first people to give my brother a hug when the team arrived at La Catedral. Despite it being a huge honor for us to have such important and renowned athletes in the jail and being able to play against them, I think it was also an honor for them to play a football match with none other than the entire Cartel de Medellin, captained by Pablo Escobar. All those activities required Inpec authorization, which is the supreme government authority within the jail system. Besides, the football teams also visited other jails around the country.

From that week onward, three additional flags flew at El Catedral next to the Colombian and Inpec flags. They were joined by the flag from El Nacional, the flag from Medellín and the flag from Envigado. Sometimes, we would have some fun and we would swap the flags. One day, for example, the El Nacional flag wasn't waiving, and instead there was a bigger Medellín flag. The following day, the Medellín flag disappeared and a giant El Nacional flag was flown in its place. At night, Pablo used to take the flags off and exchange them at 2 or 3 o'clock in the morning.

THE "WINERY" TRUCKS

After that unforgettable week, things returned to normal. Pablo returned to do his thing, which was reading, talking on the phone, and getting visits from lawyers. He talked on the phone until the early hours. I used to sit beside him in a rocking chair while he chatted. At night, the view was beautiful. You could see the fast cars through the avenues, and you could even hear the noise of their motors. The Envigado buildings lit up bit by bit, and one could imagine the families inside, eating or conversing or simply getting ready for the next day. There were clear nights with fresh air, unlike the others in which the fog covered everything. The temperatures were generally really low, and when one talked, a smoke halo came out of their mouth, as if instead of speaking, one was smoking. But neither Pablo nor I smoked. We didn't like liquor. The only alcoholic beverage that my brother used to drink, only once in a while, was Heineken beer. He also used to smoke marijuana although it was sporadic. He used to say that it allowed him to relax, especially at night. He might prepare a joint, and then throw it out before finishing it. The nights in La Catedral were all very similar. Pablo paced from side to side in the main corridor in front of the rooms, while everyone else was sleeping. Since he used to go to sleep so late, he would get up late as well the following day; sometimes two or three o'clock in the afternoon. I enjoyed looking at the landscape of what was our own jail. Pablo was right when he picked that plot of land for its safety.

Before coming to La Catedral, Pablo had information that someone wanted to aerial attack the jail with a bomb. This is why he chose a location up in the mountains, thinking that it would be difficult for a plane to get close and target La Catedral through the dense fog. He wanted a location that was surrounded by trees, both for safety, and because he loved nature. The last project that he told me about was an urbanization of an area called La Chinita in Ubará. He wanted to buy the land there so that he could plant trees and build houses for all of the people in the area. They were putting together a plan for that project, and he had already sent somebody to find out who the owner of the land was so that he could immediately start working on it. Pablo also needed the ecological work to begin as soon as possible since the plan was for the urbanization to have a lot of newly planted trees. Pablo Escobar was one of the pioneers in Medellin tree planting. Every eight days, when he wasn't travelling, he went to Medellin with a truck full of trees of every kind, and he seeded them throughout the entire city and its parks. In the secret negotiations with César Gavíría's government, as I have already stated, Pablo was very serious and underscored the fact that one of the conditions for his surrender was the prohibition of cutting down trees in the area. This would unintentionally work in our favor as one year later this would make our escape from La Catedral a whole lot easier.

But we did have some restrictions on what we could do and could not do, although football matches and visits from our lawyers were allowed. During the first few months, we devoted much of our time to designing security systems and providing for my brother's men to get the proper legal help. Friends of Pablo who were well-known within the entertainment world or within politics, didn't want their names to appear in any records which would tie them to Pablo. Models, actors, actresses, beauty queens, political leaders, artists. From jail, Pablo went on managing his business, and he created ways of providing money for personal costs, food, and maintenance of the jail.

My brother bought two trucks in Itagui; a Chevrolet and a Mazda van. Both vehicles were modified for transporting people up and down the mountain. The trucks were double covered with a secret compartment within the rear of the truck, which we called the tunnel. The people who sat in the rear typically had legal problems or simply could not give their official names in order to avoid having problems with my brother's foes. Pablo made a list of the people whom he needed to see, or people who needed to see him. One of the trucks picked people up at night in different locations of the city, and brought them to a little shop located in the foothills. We owned a store there, from where we used to coordinate our transportation plans. It was called The Winery, and from there our men monitored who came up or down the mountain road to and from La Catedral. Those late night travelers used to arrive at the winery and then they were moved to a second truck. In the back part of the truck, the hidden passengers were seated, and in the front compartment, the regular passengers would sit. The guards already knew about these drop-offs, and using a code, the driver was allowed to enter the jail. At the army checkpoints, they were simply asked about the cargo that they carried, and the driver knew he had to say, "materials, sir", and that was the code. From the winery, a special communications system, designed by myself, was built. It was an internal phone with an underground cable, which communicated directly with Pablo's room and mine. When the tunnel departed for La Catedral from the winery, they notified Pablo, and we knew who was on their way to visit us.

That's how important people in Colombia were able to speak face to face with my brother. Good people and sincere friends, as well as some two-faced people, who went on to talk badly about us after we met. In the tunnel we accommodated all of the beauty queens of the era. I think that, every nominee who participated in the

Cartagena realm of beauty travelled up the tunnel. It was funny to see them all cramped in the back cover, uncomfortable and nervous. They would visit the guys, and they all had a lot of fun. Several of them fell in love, and the visits resulted in marriages. Some famous models and actresses made that trip too, whose names I prefer to leave out in order not to damage their personal and professional lives. Many times, they slept over in La Catedral, and the following day they had breakfast and then left. They left the same way that they came in. To avoid problems, several rooms had hiding spots, which were really just large dividers, built in the middle of the bedrooms, so that we wouldn't raise any suspicion of having guests. They had every comfort in their bedrooms, with televisions and personal fridges with food and drinks. Often they slept in the rooms with their entire families when it was too late at night for them to travel back to Medellin.

THE HIDDEN TEN MILLION

The tunnel was also used for smuggling money. Pablo wanted to keep cash in case of emergency, and to pay the workers there. Bit by bit, in a matter of two weeks, he sent people to pick up dollars that he kept stored in Medellin. He bought ten milk cans of the largest type so that they could put rolls of money inside. A million dollars in rolls would fit in one can. After the dollars were placed inside the milk cans, they threw salt, sugar, rice, beans, and sometimes even fresh fish. At the checkpoints, they used to look at the milk cans, and then they allowed the drivers to continue onward. "This is food for the coming week," the workers used to tell the guards. "It's fresh fish, and I can't delay delivery or else it might go bad," they told the uniformed men, who immediately allowed them through the entrance.

Once in the jail, the food was taken away, and the cash was kept stored in the milk cans. I used to secure them with a coded padlock, and only my brother knew the code. Late at night, one of the guys would bury them within a gap in the foundation which had the exact size for them to fit vertically. Over the can, they seeded grass and flowers, and even ornamental trees. Two of the cans were left below the football arena. Over the course of two months, they buried ten cans full of money. Ten million dollars cash, without the army suspecting a thing.

Using the same system, small arms were smuggled in. Before the surrender, my brother had already taken in a person rifle, and a submachine gun arsenal. He had buried them because the jail was on his lot, behind what would eventually be our rooms. Pablo thought about everything. "Someday we will need them," he explained to me later.

THE SECOND HIGUITA'S VISIT

A few months after El Loco René initially came to La Catedral, he was back, and this time to play in a much more serious game. My brother didn't like wars, and he always held that his fight with the Government was forced upon him. Because of this, he tried to fix things by fair means, even with his worst enemies. That was the real reason for Higuita's second visit. René explained to Pablo that thanks to his fame, and with the country showing love and affection for him, he could intercede with the Rodríguez Orejuela brothers so that Pablo's problems were settled with proper dialogue and not with bombs and more killing. Pablo accepted, and René promised to talk to the two brothers. For that, he counted on García Herreros' help. But it ended up being quite frustrating for Pablo. It was clear that both Gilberto and Miguel Rodríguez were very stubborn and proud people. "You know, I really can't trust anything that these two guys are saying," Pablo explained to me later. I learned that René got to talk to them, but nothing could be negotiated at that time. Later on, other well-known mediators would help cement a peaceful arrangement between Pablo and the two brothers.

In La Catedral, we had it all. Comfort, and incredible food that was prepared by two international chefs that we used to call, affectionately, the belly brothers. We had visitors all of the time, our families, outside communication, fun, sports, safety, personal protection, weapons, and money. A large part of the time was used in judicial processes and formulating arrangements with the courts. Pablo had hired almost 30 lawyers, for his defense, my defense, and for the rest of his men. We knew that sooner or later, they would be calling us to stand before a judge and have us condemned.

We celebrated several birthdays and even marriages. In La Catedral, Tato was married, and that night the bar and disco were used for the first time. Pablo had his 42nd birthday party, and we all celebrated. All of our relatives came to visit us as well as our closest friends and some of our lawyers. It was December 1st, and the guys were preparing Christmas decorations for the jail.

Pablo didn't get up early, even on his birthday. We woke him up about two o'clock in the afternoon. He took a shower and then got dressed. He was in a really good mood. My mother gave him two Russian hats as a gift, both made of pure wool. She had brought them from Russia, on a tour that Pablo bought for her birthday. From that moment, Pablo and that hat were inseparable in La Catedral. He used to say that it was going to be his symbol, as the hat was for "Che" Guevara, or the beard for Fidel Castro. He put on one of the two black hats, and he dressed in a pair of American blue Levi jeans that they had bought for him in the USA, and a red sweater his wife bought for him in Spain. The food was specially prepared in Medellin for this occasion: stuffed turkey, caviar, chinook salmon, smoked trout and Russian salad. He hired a group of waiters to serve the guests. Around three o'clock in the afternoon, the priest, authorized by Inpec, offered a mass in the name of Pablo and all of our families. Afterwards, music of every kind played and people started drinking. Pablo had only one beer. Everyone stayed late in the chairs in the corridor. That evening, two violinists played my brother's favorite songs, including some from the Opera. That was the last day that Pablo took photos with his family. He toasted with his wife and his two children. Christmas was similar, surrounded by our families. For that special day, my mother prepared stuffed turkey. We raised a lot of balloons, but Pablo didn't want us to burn gunpowder in order to avoid any problems with the Army. We gave gifts at midnight, and each one of the workers stayed in their rooms with their families. New Years was the same.

On the morning of January, 1st, Pablo reflected on what was most important in the previous year. He was really concerned about having peace in Colombia, the levels of poverty and the high unemployment. He used to say that he tolerated poverty, but not misery. That's why he wanted to be the president of this country. People used to look for him to ask for help. Hundreds of people every day used to arrive at the main entrance to ask him for economic and spiritual help. They sent him handwritten papers asking for help for a family calamity, for a terminally ill patient, or for the food of a poor family. He read them all, he investigated them, he verified the information and he satisfied every request. Several women wrote to complain about cruel or drunk husbands, and he sent cards with practical advice and with steps to follow. He always advised to keep unity at home. He was, for a lot of people, a sort of healer.

In La Catedral, he received correspondence from all around the planet. He hired a guy to read all the letters they sent to him. Mail arrived from Japan, Taiwan, Hong Kong, Singapore, India, the USA, Italy, Czechoslovakia, Cuba, Poland, France, and from everywhere else all around the world.

One day, a man from Africa proposed a deal to him. In the letter, the man wanted to sell an elephant who turned out to be the mother of another elephant, named Margaret, that Pablo had bought years before from a circus. The man explained to my brother in the letter that the idea was for him to have the mother and the daughter together in Hacienda Napoles. He sent a picture of the animal, its specifications, schedule of care, and nutrition data.

Another time, a man offered him a deal to manage all of his money that he had made from drug trafficking. The guy told Pablo that he lived in the USA, and he had seven accounts in different banks, in which he could keep his money safe. In the letter, he sent pictures of him and his addresses, so that Pablo could verify the information.

While reflecting on the current state of Colombia, one thing that did make Pablo happy was the outcome of the negotiations with the Colombian guerrillas. That night in La Catedral, we remembered how we had the sword of the liberator, Simón Bolívar, which the M-19 had stolen in a spectacular operation.

It all had started when an insurgent group kidnapped Martha Nieves Ochoa, the sister of our friends of the Ochoa Vázquez family. Pablo thought about the creation of an armed mercenary group that would stop the rampant kidnappings, and rid the nation of the bands which had already begun to seed terror within Colombia. That's when he created the MAS, which stood for Muerte a los Secuestradores (Death to Kidnappers). Their first task was to search for Martha. The first inquires indicated that she was in the hands of the guerrillas, and that's when they approached the M-19 leaders. After several conversations, an agreement for the release was reached.

Several months later, they sent an M-19 messenger to Medellin to give a message to Pablo. The man presented a peaceful plan between their guerrilla fighters and the MAS drug dealers. "We won't mess with you and your families, and you won't mess any of us and our families," the messenger proposed. Pablo gave his word and so it would be. "There are no longer any problems between us. I am going to send one of our men to finalize this peace deal," my brother told them. The messenger travelled and both parts agreed to go on with their quiet lives, each one with his business in separate ways. From this event, a special relationship between Pablo and leaders from the insurgent group was born. They gained confidence in Pablo and they admitted he was a man of his word. "Your word is like a bond," they expressed to my brother. The same messenger got in touch with Pablo again to set a date with one of the guerilla organization's leaders. It was Iván Marino Ospina, considered the most warlike leaders of M-19. He stayed in one of the secret hiding places Pablo had in Medellin, and they became good friends. The confidence reached such a point, that he revealed one of the best kept secrets in the recent national history, the place where they had the liberator sword hidden. "Bateman took the sword before dying," Iván Marino Ospina started to tell him. He went on to explain that Bateman gave it to a female guerrilla who he absolutely trusted. She died later as well, not without having told the secret to someone else within M-19. She gave it to Iván Marino, and he kept it until that day when he met with my brother.

"Pablo, I bring you the Liberator sword as a gift," Ivan Marino told my brother. "It's proof that our word is also worthy, the same as yours. It's a solidification of our peaceful pact," the guerrilla explained to him. Pablo accepted proudly, and several days after keeping it hanging on the wall of one of his houses, he brought it to a brother-in-law to keep inside one of the hiding spots in the center of the city. The commander Iván Marino would die in a confrontation with the Army in the center of Cali. His brother in law, Mario Henao, did what Pablo asked for. A few months later, Mario was murdered in an estate in the Antioquia Mountains, in a police operation. The sword seemed to determine a tragic end for anybody who had touched it. Everyone who had it in their possession, died. After the Government and the M-19 signed a peace pact, the scandal of the Liberator sword began. Journalists, political leaders, ex-presidents, in brief, all of Colombian society, started to demand the M-19 to return the sword. That's when my brother remembered. By then, we were already in La Catedral. He ordered a man to go from cave to cave until he found the sword. Finally, he gave it to a relative of ours, to whom Pablo asked to bring it to La Catedral. They brought it up in the same little truck used to transport our money and people. Pablo recognized it immediately. We all saw it, and we had the privilege to hold it in our hands. Pablo returned it again to Medellin. He got in touch with two M-19 leaders in Medellin. Their names were Martha and Álvaro. Pablo sent them a letter telling them the story of the sword. The two guerrillas received the valuable and historic national symbol, and they sent it to their leaders in Bogota, so that they could hand it over to the Government.

But Martha Nieves wasn't the only person close to us who was a powerful M-19 leader. They reminded my brother that Carlos Lehder had kidnapped in 1980 and was still in captivity. A renowned drug dealer in Medellin asked my brother to help him set Lehder free. Pablo had not yet met Ledher, but he did know that Lehder was a big drug dealer. Pablo organized a group of six men, headed by Otoniel González and composed of some gang members like chiquilín, his brother Eduardo, Santiago Maya and the family. My brother already had information that the M-19 had Lehder held hostage in a house in Armenia, which is the capital of Quindio. The group travelled to Quindio in two cars, and after two days of searching the entire city, he found the house where Lehder was kept hostage by the guerrillas. When the kidnapers knew about the presence of a group sent by my brother, they escaped through the back of the house in a Simca brand car, taking Lehder in the trunk. Lehder had luck on his side because as the car swerved to avoid an obstacle in the street, the car turned over. Lehder opened the trunk door, got out of the car and ran, but one of the kidnappers shot him in the leg. For his ransom, the M-19 demanded a sum of $5 million dollars from Lehder's friends. Pablo's men didn't pay any ransom money, and instead they captured two of the M-19 guerrillas.

Kidnapping was a very personal and touchy subject for Pablo because at one point, our own father had been kidnapped. This is why Pablo used so many resources to help free Ledher. Not even our own father, Abel Escobar, was able to escape from his kidnapers. What happened to our father was a group composed by four active policemen from Medellin, two retired ones and two civilians, took him while he was going to visit one of his estates near La Ceja village, Antioquia. My father was riding in his red Toyota van, when six men who were travelling in another truck, spoke with my father, and the next thing he knew, they had tied up his workers and then they tied him up by his hands and legs. The kidnappers demanded the sum of $50 million dollars for releasing my father. Pablo came up with a very clever way of rescuing him. He put one camera in each of 250 drugstores in Medellin, and he would use the cameras to see who might be purchasing a specific type of heart medication that our father needed because he had just had heart surgery and he used a pacemaker. For each picture the drugstores gave him, Pablo paid a reward of 5 million pesos. That's how he managed to find two of the kidnappers, who lived in Medellin. But he decided not to capture them because preferred to watch them instead. At the same time, he allocated 300 transistor radios among his friends and workers in the city, and through a radio station friend of his, he sent a coded message at the moment in which the authorities registered any incoming calls to our mother's house, whose phone was tapped. The code was, "this track is dedicated to Luz Marina, it's called Sonaron Cuatro Balazos (Four shots sounded), and it's sung by Antonio Aguilar." When Pablo's friends heard this on the radio, they would then search for the nearest public phones to know from which part of the city the calls were being made. If the area matched with the authorities' report on my mother's wire tapped telephone, then it would be easy to identify the kidnappers on the phone. Meanwhile, I was negotiating with the kidnappers, to whom I offered $10 million dollars, but they wouldn't accept. Pablo gave me instructions to make a new offer, now 200 million pesos. The idea was to stall the kidnappers, and buy us more time until we found the site where they kept my father locked away. By then, we already knew it was the same group of captors, who had kidnapped another friend of ours, and we knew some the Antioquia sites where they hid their victims. After 18 days in captivity, one of the kidnappers called me to accept Pablo's offer. We arranged a site in Medellin to bring them the 200 million pesos in cash, but before packing those bills in a bag, my brother threw in some tracking devices bought from the USA, very similar to the ones used to locate stolen cars. The next thing that we did was follow the captors up to an estate located in the mountains of a town called Liborina, about 150 kilometers from Medellin. A group of our men were already waiting for the arrival of the captors with the money, and our men followed them to a small house built into the ridge of the mountain. The men, hired by my brother, entered the house through several places. They captured three of the kidnappers, and my father was freed.

Another time my favorite horse was kidnapped, Terremoto de Manizales (Manizales Earthquake). He is considered one of the best Paso Fino horses of the world. The authorities' persecution of this animal was almost as bad as the persecution that they did to us. Their orders were to find my horse and seize him. That's why I kept him hidden in some Medellin stables, and there they came to take him away one morning. He was gone for 20 days, after which he appeared tied to a tree beside the avenue known as La Guacatala, in El Poblado neighborhood. They returned him castrated and visibly mistreated, dehydrated, and with signs of not having eaten any food. We recovered him, and I still keep him in one of the stables of an estate in Caldas. He reached a price of $2 million dollars. Being just a colt, he beat two world champions in an international race. Nowadays, his sons are spread among several European countries, Central America, and in North America, and each horse is priced between $800,000 to $1,000,000 dollars.

La Catedral was often a very tense environment, and will forever remain a significant part of the lives of everybody who stayed there, as well as for our children, our wives, and our mothers. Today, I have to admit that it was in La Catedral where I learned more about my brother than at any other moment. Being in La Catedral afforded us the time to reflect on our lives because we did not have to fear being attacked or threatened by the Government or other cartels.

THE ESCAPE

The day of the escape, Pablo woke up earlier than ever. Those two days were the only ones, as far as I can remember, in which he didn't get up late, as his custom was. That day, he had an appointment with doctor Uribe at nine o'clock in the morning. He had made an important decision: to confess the crimes he had actually committed, which included bombings, kidnappings, and killings.

He had been reflecting for quite some time. One night he took me by my arm and he told me, "Brother, there are things we must face, however painful they may seem." It was one of the few times I saw his face filled with regret. As a man of his word, Pablo wasn't afraid of anything, let alone the truth. He was willing to confess his crimes to the Government and to the country. He was aware that many people disliked his war with the state, but he also believed that they misunderstood him. According to him, opinions were divided. "Look, brother, I know there are people who don't agree with my ideas, but I want the country and the world to understand that, in a seemingly strange way, I have actually been forced to do most of things that I've done," he told me that night.

My brother regretted the deaths of many innocent people. Despite most people around the world viewing his as a monster, for me, for his family, for his children and for many Colombians, Pablo Escobar was a good human being that was a gift to Colombia. Today, thousands of people come from many parts of the country to visit his grave. To cry for him. They treat him like a saint, they light candles for him and worship him. We've found letters from humble people asking him to bring them luck so that they can win the lottery, or an opportunity that takes them away from all of the poverty once and for all. Also messages from women who had been lied to and abandoned by their boyfriends or husbands, asking Pablo to return them soon to their empty hearts. People who have come from all around the world, take pictures of themselves beside his grave. On December 2nd, on the anniversary of his death is the mass of Mount Sacro, where he was buried, a huge mass is attended by other dead people's bereaved, who prefer to cry for my brother instead.

Many of the crimes which the courts and the Government have attributed to Pablo, weren't actually committed by him. They blamed him, and made him known for being a murderer and a terrorist, while the criminals were actually his enemies. People, who I will not mention by name because the only thing that we want is whatever peace we have achieved for the country to remain. We forgive all of them, and we pray to God for them to also forgive us of everything. The chapter is closed, and the wounds are healing.

Let's get back to how Pablo's day started. He would let doctor Uribe know that he wanted an appointment at nine o'clock. The lawyer came to the meeting and locked himself in a room with my brother. I was present in that meeting, but about half an hour later, we received the first warning. We had a special communication system all along the jail's roof. Radios were installed at different points, which were connected in turn, to a main radio in our control. We had the first contact point way below, the little estate that also belonged to us, which was called *The winery*. I had bought it and given it to *Tato* as a gift, one of Pablo's workers, the day of his marriage in La Catedral. There, inside the little house, was an underground phone. Something like an intercom with the cable buried, which I had installed long before. It was about three kilometers long, and on each end of it another phone. From there, the guys used to talk to us without any risk of our communications being intercepted. Upstairs, in the jail, each one of us had another phone. Pablo had one in his room, I had another one in mine, and there was another phone where one of our guards was. The first one to receive the call was a guard of ours who was supposed to be on alert for calls 24 hours a day. He used to forward it to me, or if I wasn't there, he forwarded it to Pablo. So, when it was about 15 minutes to 10, one of our workers called from below and told us there were a lot of soldiers on their way up and they had even seen the Fourth Brigade commander himself, General Pardo Ariza. According to the guy who called us, they have already brought up like three trucks. "You have to be really careful," he told Pablo through the intercom. Later we were warned that someone from the Government was about to come up and talk to us. At twelve noon, the Vice Minister of Justice and the Prison's director, who was Colonel Navas, drove up. When they arrived, they asked for my brother at once, they explained that they had instructions from the president to be allowed to let the Army come in for a requisition.

"I am very sorry, gentlemen, but I have negotiated a compromise with Gaviría's Government, and neither the Police nor the Army can enter this jail," my brother told me in a good tone, because he never used dirty language or insulted people. "If you want, bring Inpec guards to look through everything we have here, but I warn you that I won't let the Army in, let alone the Police, he emphasized. Remember, gentlemen," he insisted, that I already endured a long war with the Police, and that's the deal."

I saw the Vice Minister, and he looked really worried. A rather young guy, thin and who looked like an undergraduate. From the beginning, he looked nervous and above all, inexperienced. The man walked a few meters away and started to call President Gaviría. They talked for a while and he told him that Pablo didn't want to allow for the requisition to be carried out. My brother saw the Vice Minister Mendoza so worried that he offered to let the Army in, but with the soldiers disarmed. The Vice Minister and Colonel Navas accepted and Mister Mendoza called President Gaviría again, but the President did not accept those conditions. "The president insists on letting the Army inside, but armed. If not, there's no deal."

So Pablo warned them, "No, brother, I won't let them in like this. Here we will be killed, and they're not entering in here with weapons because they'll kill us for sure!"

The Vice Minister and the Colonel told him not to take things to that point, and told us to try to find a rapid and trouble-free solution to the issue. But my brother had already decided not to give up. "We don't know what your intentions are. I've had a long and hard-fought war against the Government, and I'm not going to let you kill me," he warned in a louder tone.

So we all knew that things were heating up and about to go totally crazy. About four o'clock in the afternoon, after several incoming and outcoming calls, the Government started to make a few mistakes. They took away the military cordon which had been set by General Pardo with troops from the Fourth Brigade. They called us from below to tell us that they have started to bring up trucks with new soldiers from Bogota in Hércules trucks, which we learned from our contacts in the capital of the country that they had departed from Catam military airport and from Palanquero base in Salgar Port. The planes were arriving at both airports: Olaya Herrera and Rionegro. The army's mistake was that they brought in soldiers from Bogota who didn't know the area very well. "We're going to sleep and tomorrow we will come back to see how we can fix this. Tomorrow we will go up."

In that moment, Pablo received a call from an Army General in which they informed him to be very careful because Pablo's life was in imminent danger. The Army's intentions were to come in, kill or capture Pablo and then have him extradited. I will omit his name because he's still an active General, and I don't want to put his family in harm's way. The General again cautioned Pablo to be careful and said that, if he was able to call him again later, he would give more details or he would find out the Army's true intentions. Now Pablo was very worried, because the information was given by a fully trusted General, who was a friend of many years, and we had to trust him. "This is crazy, brother," he told me as he stepped aside from the two Government officials.

The next moment, we were in the jail director's house, which was the first house after the main entrance to La Catedral. It was then that my brother made the decision not to let the Colonel and the Vice Minister leave. "I'm going to ask you a favor, please do not leave the jail," he told them. Both looked at each other, and didn't know how to answer. Pablo explained what he had just said, "It's for the safety and for the lives of everyone of us. I am forced to keep you retained while a solution for this is found." Vice Minister Mendoza and Colonel Navas turned pale. They called Nariño's House several times, but we didn't know what they were told from Bogota.

The situation intensified as we started to hear planes. Pablo told them that he wanted to speak personally with President Gaviria, but they would not bring the phone to Pablo. Mendoza also wanted to tell Gaviria to talk to my brother Pablo, but they would not hand the phone to the Vice Minister either. The only one to whom we spoke with was the private secretary, I think he was a Doctor Silva.

Pablo talked to him and so did Vice Minister Mendoza. They agreed they would talk again, and after that the conversation was cut off. Pablo and the Vice Minister insisted, but Doctor Silva wasn't calling us back and it seemed that President Gaviría was determined not to speak with anybody at La Catedral.

We were all tense. Seeing that there was no solution with the Government in sight, I decided to take one of my plans into action. In the middle of October, I had ordered to buy cable cutting shears from an Envigado ironworks. They were strong enough to cut through high-caliber wires. I left Pablo and the others in the director's house, and I came to the west part of the main building, that is to say behind, in the upper part, in the green zone. I didn't want anyone else to go with me. When I passed by the tool warehouse, I took out an iron bar specially made for breaking up soil. With it in hand, I walked a few meters above, where months ago I had left the cable cutters buried very deep. Only my brother and I knew about this spot. As I had prior knowledge about the military guard shift change, I took advantage of when there was no guard present. The only soldiers who could be seen from where I was were about 80 meters away, and the thick fog provided poor visibility so they couldn't see me. With the bar, I dug up the shears, and I went up through the steepest part of the plot, beside the main wire fence. With Pablo, we had made a lot of changes to that part of the jail, and we concluded that it was the perfect location in case of an emergency like the one that we were currently in. It was a strategic place, because exactly below the wire fence, there was a gorge which had formed a sort of tunnel, with enough room for one normal-sized person to fit. My brother and I were convinced that it was the only place in the entire 30,000 square meter jail that we would someday use to breakout. Using the shears, I broke the wires with great difficulty, making a hole in the wire fence about one meter wide.

Meanwhile, according to what I was told later, in the director's house, they were all very nervous, especially Colonel Navas Rubio, the Inpec national director. In the middle of despair, he asked for whisky to calm his nerves. Vice Minister Mendoza asked for coffee. Both of them were assisted. The Colonel stepped up from his chair and said, "This could be the last whisky I drink in my life." The man was really distressed, and his face was totally pale. Minutes later, he approached an altar which the jail director had made beside the hall, and took a Bible opened to Psalm 91. He leaned down solemnly before the Bible, and he took some time to read the Psalm. Later, with his face distorted, he came back to us and asked to make a phone to call. Popeye, who was the one in charge of guarding them, asked him what he needed the phone for, and the colonel confessed he wanted to say goodbye to his family. "I think I'm gonna die," he sentenced. Later, with a faltering voice, he told us stories about his life in the Army, and he confessed that when he was called to travel to the jail, no one told him what the mission was. "I put on my uniform when I was on the plane. I didn't know anything," he expressed.

I had already created the hole in the wire fence, and I returned to the director's house, after storing the shears in the warehouse.

I joined the group just at the moment in which Pablo was telling Popeye and El Angelito to take the people to his room. "Let's take them hostage right now," my brother ordered. Right then, five of the guys took them to the alcove, located at the end of the corridor. During that route, my brother stayed in my room, located close to his. I kept going with the three hostages. There was no need to threaten or tie them up, although almost everyone, except me, was carrying a weapon. There were AR-15's, MAC-10 machine pistols, mini uzis, handguns, and a shotgun. Pablo had brought those weapons to La Catedral long before his surrender, and he had placed them very carefully in a cave, which only he had knowledge of. Within the group, the only one who had two different weapons was Pablo: an Uzi hanging from his right arm, and on his belt he was carrying the famous Sig Sauer, a 9 millimeter handgun, which at that time was used exclusively in the German Army. A military friend from Germany had sent it to him as a special gift. Despite the powerful armament, everything seemed pretty peaceful. We accommodated them in some easy chairs in the hall of Pablo's bedroom, and they were offered food and something to drink. The three of them drank coffee. They looked even more nervous now, surely in light of the fact that the Government hadn't answered any of their calls, and there were planes flying over the area, though at high altitudes. I asked *Popeye* for the radiophone, and I tuned into the same frequency as my brother. It was on channel 113. He asked me about the hostages, and I told him that all of them were still in the room. So he advised me to lower the window curtains. I figured out what Pablo's intention was: To be able to pass by the alcove's window overlooking the corridor without being seen by the hostages. At that moment, an Air Force airplane had flew at a lower altitude than the rest. We knew because we all heard the motors from our room. So I decided to use my emergency action plan. About three months after the voluntary submission into the jail, I thought about a system that would allow us to have the switches of all the lights in La Catedral under our control. I installed some switches in some strategic places. One of them in the end of Pablo's room, and the other in a bunker, which I also ordered to be built on the upper floor of the building.

I walked to the end of the room, and I went to the external wall of the corridor, where the switch was. I flipped the switch, and the whole jail went dark. Everybody was really nervous at this point, even our guards. One of them, Sander, went out, and told us the hostages were panicking. I told the guard to tell them to calm down, that it was simple a safety measure because of the planes flying overhead. That was the only thing that they asked us. Then Pablo showed up, and told me to enter the room with the hostages.

He tried to calm them down, and he insisted that they shouldn't worry about the lights going out. So he proposed to them that we all go back to the director's house. They accepted joyfully. We went out again through the corridor, and we entered the house. We insisted on an immediate phone call with the President. Pablo was still looking to have a dialogue, and it just wasn't going to happen. Neither Gavíria nor his subordinates picked up the phone, and it's possible that they were not yet inside Nariño Palace. Pablo tried several times through his mobile phone, and he didn't get an answer either. The cold was getting more intense and the fog thicker.

There was a moment of absolute silence in which only some cicadas and birds were heard, and once in a while the yelling of a soldier outside. Several people among those present were carrying transistor radios, and were on alert for any news, which was now beginning to spread around the world. The different radio stations were talking about an armed takeover of La Catedral, with many dead and wounded. Others speculated that Pablo had already been extradited and flown to Florida in a DEA plane. Every report talked about a military presence in the jail, confirming once again what his friend, the General, had already told him. I saw my brother Pablo walking away from the group towards the corridor of the jail director's house. He made me a sign with his eyes, and I followed him. He took out the mobile phone from the suitcase and he dialed his wife's house. He talked to his children Manuela and Juan Pablo, and later to his wife, María Victoria. I heard he was also calming them down, since they were also listening to the radio stations which talked about a military incursion with bloodshed and fire. "Don't worry, we are OK, ignore the news. This is all being created by the President Gaviria," he told them."

I did the same. I called my sons Nicolás and José Roberto. Then we dialed my mother and, together, both Pablo and myself, talked to her and we calmed her down. My brother called Father García Herreros and told him what was happening and about the Government's intentions. He told him that nobody had made things clear or wanted to tell him what was actually happening. The Father promised he would get in touch with President Gaviría, but this was useless too. Nobody explained what was happening. That's the moment when Pablo decided to run away. Cesar Gaviría had not fulfilled the deal that they had made for his surrender. Running away was, at that moment, the only possible way out after so many attempts to fix the situation. Pablo never thought about running away. We didn't have any other alternatives anymore. "Either we run away, or we all get killed here," he warned us. We knew that running away was also risking death because the surroundings of the jail were guarded by more than two thousand soldiers willing to shoot at anything that moved in the middle of the darkness. At approximately 1:30 in the morning, the planes kept flying overhead and, according to the information my brother had received by phone from an air controller, in Olaya Herrera de Medellin, some Air Force helicopters brought from Bogota were present. The situation was really suspenseful, and we were nervous. Pablo went towards the rooms and started to gather people. I stayed with the hostages, guarded by *Popeye*. Not everyone, who had surrendered in La Catedral, decided to run away. However it was already clear that my brother was definitely going to run. He chose to take his men in the best physical condition, and he knew which ones were in good shape from the football matches. Besides, some of them were pretty overweight, and others had health problems, fractures or broken limbs. For example, Valentín de Jesús Taborda, had suffered from a serious leg injury, product of three shots that he received in the rescue operation of Andrés Pastrana Arango, later elected President of the Republic. So, Taborda wasn't able to take part in the operation.

Pablo always wore tennis shoes, generally white and with metal spikes, Adidas-brand. He wore them with loose laces. In our evening talks, he used to comment that the day we saw him tying his tennis shoes, it would be because an emergency was approaching. It was like the equivalent of alarm bells going off. Pablo called out for me, and I went to the site where he had gathered with the other guys. "I've already picked the people who are coming with us," he said, and then he bent over to tie his laces. We all looked at each other, and Gustavo González, one of the people chosen for the breakout, told me, "Brother, this is getting serious, the boss is tying his shoes." I looked at Pablo, who was still tying the lace of his left shoe, and he told me, "Roberto, let's change the radio frequency, put yours on the same frequency as mine." So we knew that those were the last minutes that we had left inside the famous La Catedral jail. He explained to me that the plan consisted of coming out one by one, so that we wouldn't arouse suspicion among the hostages and the prison guards. My brother took *El Angelito* first.

That's how we called Alfonso León Puerta Muñoz, one of the young men most beloved by my brother, trusted and, above all, in excellent physical condition. He took him out through the hole that I already created, and he told him to scout out the spot through which we would have to depart. *El Angelito* returned a moment later with a good report that the ground was in good condition, and the darkness, the fog and the rain would make it difficult for the soldiers to see us, even though the soldiers were just a few meters away from the mesh. Pablo still remained inside the jail, beside the mesh, and through the radiophone he was asking me to send out another one of our men every three or four minutes. Meanwhile, *Popeye* arrived to where I was located, and he told me that the hostages stayed with the group of guys who weren't going to run away. They remained in the house of the jail director.

Pablo had given a code for me to dispatch the people, "Get me a coffee, and some soap, throw me a towel, I already finished taking a shower." One of the last of our men was Popeye, who had given instructions to our men that remained with the hostages, to make sure that the hostages were well entertained. In this way, they wouldn't notice that we were leaving the jail. Before my exit, Pablo and I decided to go to the director's house again so that the hostages would see us and not suspect anything. Pablo told them he was going to sleep for a while, and if anything happened they could wake him up, in case they managed to talk to the Government. He insisted on them to be quiet, and that the idea was to get everything solved with no need for any bloodshed. He got away from the house, and he went back to the mesh wire fence again. I stayed with the hostages a little longer. Standing in front of them, I talked to Pablo through the radiophone, and I let the hostages know that Pablo had already gone to bed. Later when I left the room, I told them that I was also going to sleep. I felt calm, with no fear or anxiety, but I did think a lot about my family because they were probably more worried than I was. I went to my room, and I changed the tennis shoes that I used to wear for a pair of wellington boots, special for the rough terrain which was waiting for us. I took a jacket, I changed the radiophone batteries, and I picked up a small transistor to listen to the news. I also picked up a National-brand mobile phone I used to keep stored under the bed, and which weighed about five kilos. Once in a while I communicated with the guys that were taking care of the hostages, and I told the Vice Minster that I would come back in an hour after getting some sleep. They already knew where to find me if anything happened. Before coming out, I took a rain jacket from the closet, because it was really cold and the rain was coming down. Also a helmet, like the kind that I used when I was a cyclist, which had a logo for the brand *Bicicletas El Osito* ("The Little Bear Bicycles"). I understood that I was taking longer than expected, and Pablo had already started bugging me to leave. He messaged me constantly through the radiophone. I slowly walked through the corridor. I looked for the city below, with the hope of seeing for the last time, from La Catedral, my beloved Medellin. I didn't find it. Everything was covered in thick fog. In that moment, I realized that the 396 special days of my life were now coming to an end; an incredible chapter, full of happy moments. A place where I learned to understand life better, to see it in a different way, to reflect on the situation in my country, to understand the importance of my family. In addition, I shared this unique time with my brother, Pablo, which consisted of the most sincere moments of his life.

I went towards the site of the mesh wire where Pablo was. There was so much fog that I couldn't see or identify anyone, even two meters away. For a moment, I lost my way, and I couldn't dare whistle because I was afraid to be heard by the soldiers. I will admit that in that particular moment, I started panicking. I was alone and in despair, I thought that everyone had already gone, and left me behind. But a moment later I calmed down, because I knew that Pablo, my brother, would never leave me alone. He would be willing to give his life for me. He always insisted that if it was for me, he would let them kill him instead. I arrived at the fence, and a few meters away I saw what looked liked our guys. It was my brother and the others! I was sure that, if I stayed in the jail, I would have been killed just for being Pablo's brother. Everyone had already passed through the mesh. I went through the hole, and I moved over to where they rest of them were waiting. It was 1:50 in the morning. At that moment, the famous run from La Catedral began. We were already fugitives. We knew what to expect, because the fatigue we would get from going down the Rocky Mountains would add to the difficulty of moving through this cold temperature, which many times felt like sharp knifes entering our nose. It was clear to us that the trek down the mountain must be slow. First, to save energy and second, not to arouse any suspicion. Besides, any false step could put our lives in danger, for a fall or a slip against the huge rocks that appeared to fall down over us. The first obstacle was precisely a giant flat rock which looked like a natural wall. To go over it, we made a human staircase. The tallest and best-built were below, and over their shoulders were the smaller ones. The ones who reached the top, helped the others and so on. The first one to reach the top was *El Tato* Avendaño, after him, *El Mugre* came up and third, *El Angelito*. Pablo and I were the last ones. A thick, dark and wet forest was waiting for us. The place was inhabited by giant sharp ferns, and there was no place to pass by. We had to build a human train. One after the other, grabbing each other's hands and feet, we went through about 150 meters dragging ourselves through the mud. At that moment, we actually had no idea where we were going, because visibility was still terrible. I think we kept circling around the same place for a long time, without getting any further. We arrived at a place with less rocks, without any trees or ferns. It was a small paddock, and when we looked left we found a big surprise; La Catedral was still in front of our noses, only about 400 meters away in a straight line. We felt disappointed for a moment, because we had spent almost 2 hours running away, and it looked like we hadn't moved forward. We were sitting ducks for snipers from La Catedral. Pablo tried to encourage us to keep going, and he rushed us to go down faster, now that the forest was less difficult to move through. Besides, we had seven guys in the group actually wearing Army camouflage, and if anything happened they would likely be confused with other soldiers, and they wouldn't shoot at us. The strong wind helped to improve the visibility. Sometimes, while lying on the ground, we could see the shadows of the soldiers guarding the site, about 200 meters away.

Pablo had a really good sense of location. Everyone of us knew the area very well, but especially my brother, who walked that place since he was a little boy, when my mother, who was a teacher at that time, lived with us in La Paz neighborhood in Envigado.

At that moment, my brother Pablo became our guide. It was four in the morning, and we hurried up the steps in view of the upcoming sunrise. Pablo said that we must reach the highway and arrive to a safe place before six o'clock. With daylight breaking, anybody who found us along the way would recognize us. We started moving down the hill much faster, and began to see a few houses in Envigado. It's called *La Chocolatera* (*The Chocolate Maker*) and it belongs to *El Salado* neighborhood (*The Salty*). Looking backwards to the upper part of the mountain, La Catedral could be seen about 2,000 meters away in a straight line. It felt surreal that after we put in so much effort and almost four hours, La Catedral was still there. It was almost as if it was touching our backs, like a giant ghost who kept watching and chasing after us. We finally arrived at the bottom of the hill. It was daytime. The sun was threatening us as if it had become an ally to the same soldiers who kept chasing us. Around that time, almost six, people in Envigado came out to buy food for breakfast, and children started going to class. For the rest of humanity, it was a run-of-the-mill day. For us, it was like the end of the world or the revival of our lives. We gambled everything for everything. People looked at us as if we were ghosts or dead bodies that just come out of our graves in a horror movie, and children approached us with the look of being scared and at the same time with a childish curiosity. The elders who passed by us didn't even raise their faces to look at us, and others greeted us like the old neighbors who had just come back. We looked like a group of ragged men who were dirty, with mud in their beards, sweating profusely, looking like sick medical patients who smelled bad like the crazy people who had just been released from the local psychiatric hospital. The hunger pangs that started at 3 o'clock in the morning seemed to be reinforced even more by that appearance of being homeless to which any parishioner would be willing to give a coin for God's charity. Only a few recognized us in the middle of all of the uncertainty, and the fear of meeting face to face with the man who was at that moment starting to become the most wanted human being on the planet.

Pablo remembered that, just by chance, a few blocks away there was the house of an old friend. Memo Pérez, who was one of my brother's workers, and he was the same man who once lent us his house to stay at overnight, after my brother ran away from El Bizcocho estate (*The Biscuit*), in a different military operation. Memo worked with my brother in the drug business. He was one of the people in charge of getting the hiding spots ready and making the stocklists and coordinating the dispatches for the airstrips. The Memo estate was called *La Cilguera*, after the bird with the same name; very abundant in the area known as Alto de la Pava, where the house had been built.

We knocked on the door and Raúl, the buttler, opened it with the look of terror in his face. Some neighbors recognized us and saw us entering the friend's house. Pablo didn't get too worried, because all those people loved my brother very much, and he was sure no one would betray him. Raúl made us enter through the hall, and that was the first time we had a chance to rest. Half an hour later, someone knocked on the door. We all got worried, and several of the guys got ready with their weapons behind the doors, expecting a military platoon. Raúl opened the door, and to our surprise there were the neighbors of that entire block who were bringing breakfast already prepared. Chocolate pots, hot milk, just baked *arepas,* and country scrambled eggs with onion and tomato. We graciously ate like pigs, and received that gesture of affection to Pablo and to all of us. We knew, more than ever, that we could also count on them. They became our sentinels. They placed themselves on the corners to watch for the arrival of soldiers, and to warn us immediately. Pablo and I took our shirts, socks and jackets off, all of which were unrecognizable because of the dirt and mud from the mountain.

A neighbor picked up our clothes, and she took them to her house to wash them. We then cleaned off our feet, and we trembled from the cold. We took a good cold shower with a hosepipe that was coming down from the mountain gorge. I shaved with an old blade covered with mold which I found in the bathroom. We waited for a while until they gave us back our clothes, which were already clean but still wet. Pablo and I dressed up. We were as good as new. The only thing missing was that Cartier lotion I always carried, which this time I couldn't take with me. I felt uncomfortable without pouring something on my face after that shave, so I took a bottle of alcohol, I stirred it with water and I added a jasmine flower that I pulled out from the garden. I whipped the bottle and prepared a homemade lotion which I threw on immediately. Others who had shaved too, begged me to let them use it. Everyone tried it. It was eight o'clock in the morning. I took the mobile phone I brought from the jail, and everyone called home to calm down our loved ones who hadn't heard any news from us in hours. We told them not to believe what the radio said, and that we were already safe. We told them not to tell anyone anything, and that we would call again during the night.

I asked Pablo how he felt, and he told me that he was great. I looked at his eyes, and I just didn't believe him. He never felt sick. In fact, he never visited a doctor, and he never had his blood tested. He had enviable health, he never had any problems with his teeth, since he took almost a half an hour everyday brushing them.

The radios were on now, and every radio station kept talking about the takeover of La Catedral by the Army, according to an order by President Gaviría. It was already being talked about in the news that the takeover had resulted in the death of the guard commander, Sargent Mina, because he had supposedly resisted. Months later, Sander, the young guard friend of ours at La Catedral, would tell me the truth about what had happened. According to Sander's story, around seven in the morning of the following day, General Gustavo Pardo Ariza, commander of the Fourth Brigade of the Army, gave the order to enter La Catedral shooting and with explosive devices. Troops came in through the main entrance and shouted, "Everyone to the floor!" Everyone obeyed except Sargent Mina, who was in the main entrance. The young guard, of dark complexion and indigenous to Guachene, Cauca, tried to run away. Shots were heard, and when we raised our heads, we saw him lying on the floor. The soldiers were already in the main waiting room, before the corridor where the cells were. There was a gate with a lock. The uniformed soldiers broke the lock and entered by force. They insisted on being taken to Pablo and to the hostages. No one said anything. Actually, the hostages had been taken to Pablo's room after the escape, around five in the morning. In view of everyone's silence and nobody giving the location of Pablo, the soldiers started to run like crazy through the main corridor, opening every room by force, with explosives and bombs. When they reached Pablo's room, they found the hostages and the guys who could not make the escape attempt. Everyone was lying on the floor when the military men entered. The Vice Minister stood up immediately and rose with his arms in the air shouting, "Don't shoot, don't shoot, I'm the Justice Vice Minister." The hostages were released and Pablo's workers were captured. They also took the municipal guards and the Inpec guards to prison. All of the uniformed soldiers were confused. Even though they had already released the hostages, the main objective hadn't been accomplished. They kept asking for Pablo, and in every room they entered, they shot the mattress thinking he was hiding under the bed.

But at that time, while they searched for him in the bedrooms, my brother, myself, and his men, were enjoying good coffee and the news radio broadcast from Memo Pérez's house.

Once in a while we leaned out the window, and we saw the helicopters buzzing over our heads, and even the little soldiers in the helicopter gunships were visible from the house where we were.

Seeing that the military operation looked very serious and in full force, we devised a strategy to entertain the military men in La Catedral, and avoid being searched in the houses of Envigado. We knew at that moment it was impossible to come out on the streets and keep walking. Pablo said it was better to stay in the house and wait until night time. I talked with him about my plan, he liked it and he immediately agreed. Right then, I called my son Nicolás through the radiotelephone. I quickly gave him a new radio frequency for him to change the radio to. I told him to remember the birth date of the small boy, who was riding the yellow motorbike, and lived in La Francia neighborhood in Manizales. I explained that the first number of the new code was the month of birth and the second number, the day of birth. He understood that I was talking about his own birthday, which was on June 21st. The new frequency through which we were to talk on was 621. I warned him that in an emergency, we would return to channel 113, where we were currently talking. But that wasn't necessary. I gave him instructions to call a radio station with national coverage and say that Pablo and the rest of us were still inside La Catedral, in a tunnel we had built months ago. That we were heavily armed, and with enough ammunition for a week, and with food and water for a month. That we would be ok dying, and we are looking for a peaceful way out of this situation. Furthermore, we request the presence of a Government commission and the Prosecution so that we can surrender voluntary.

Nicolás complied with it to the letter. A moment later, we heard it directly on a radio station from Caracol, giving an interview to the journalist Darío Arizmendi, who believed the story and asked for details about the fake tunnel and everything else. The news, of course, was heard in La Catedral by the high military command, who changed the operation and directed their forces to search for a tunnel in the jail where they believed Pablo and the others were. With special machines they had brought from the Brigade, they took almost an entire day digging up the soil at La Catedral.

"The only thing they're gonna find is the money in the milk cans," Pablo told us while leaning out through the window and looking up at the mountain. He didn't care about the loss of $10 million dollars, and he never told us to try and get that money back. Later we came to the conclusion that the military must have found the money, but perhaps not all of it. Maybe some of the cans still remain buried around the jail.

Our stay in the little house in Envigado was peaceful for us. We had time to sleep and play cards, and we had creole chicken *sanchoco*. About five o'clock, I called José Fernando Posada Fierro from the mobile phone, a direct employee of my brother, whom Pablo really trusted and appreciated. He had met him in Hacienda Napoles. After my cousin, Gustavo Gaviría's death, José Fernando became my brother's right hand, and the man who started to manage the office from which Pablo directed his drug dealing business. José Fernando was about 1.78 meters tall, almost 80 kilos in weight, very talkative, especially when it came to horses and farming.

I called him, and I entrusted him with the following mission. I told him in code to search for the friend that I used to go jogging with before I made my surrender. I referred to *El Negro* Nelson (*The Black Man*), a guy who used to fix my boats and motorboats when I was devoted to water sports. I really trusted his family. I explained to José Fernando that he should tell *El Negro* to pick up three cars that had radios. We were going to be there between twelve midnight and one o'clock in the morning at the site that I had already given him using the special code. I explained that he should look for an iron door, which served as an entrance to an estate of some gentlemen whose last name was Arango, where El Negro and I used to finish our jogs. It was placed over the highway that was being built to go to Alto Las Palmas, on the same route that led to the airport.

While I was talking to José Fernando, the others were all watching television. At six in the evening, when there were planes and helicopters still flying overhead, Pablo gave the order to build a new runaway. We drank cold coffee, we put on our jackets, we had something to eat, and we got ready to leave at seven when the planes and helicopters weren't heard anymore.

The house was located beside the main road. We went out together through the back part, and we took a road across the forest. We reached the part where the mountains started, in the middle of estate houses and paddocks with animals. The idea was to cross the mountain to reach the main avenue, which goes from Envigado to Alto de Las Palmas. We were all very calm and Popeye kept bringing up dirty jokes that made everyone laugh. On a few occasions, the laughter made us fall over, because of the silly things that he got away with. Otoniel González, known as *Otto*, saw an estate on the steep part of the mountain, and told Pablo that we should go there. We were already close to Loma El Escobero, which was on the way to Las Palmas. It was *Chepe Volqueta*'s estate, who was another employee of Pablo. The butler let us in, after recognizing Otto. When he saw Pablo, he asked about the tunnel, and my brother laughed. In the house there was a normal landline telephone, and we all called our families. We screamed, *"Long live freedom,"* because the site was really safe, and we were close to the extraction point where José Fernando and El Negro were waiting for us in the cars. The butler prepared food for us, and he even made the beds, thinking that we were going to stay. Pablo talked to our mother, and he re-confirmed that the cars had been dispatch to pick us up. He was told that the site was clear of any soldiers and policemen. We went out again. From there we could see La Catedral, and we could also hear the explosions from the dynamite, which they used in the search for the tunnel. We turned our focus back to walking towards the highway where the cars were waiting for us. Amid the calm mood that we were in, as we were passing by an estate, five German shepherd dogs came out and chased us for a while. They actually bit Carlos Aguilar Gallego, *El Mugre*. But no one dared shoot their guns in the air to chase away the animals because the noise could give us away. My brother Pablo took some candy out of his jacket pocket, and threw them at the dogs. It was the only way to calm them down. One of the dogs got closer to Pablo, and he let him stroke his head and his snout. Pablo told us to keep walking slowly while he entertained the animals. He always had a solution for everything. Around 1:30 in the morning, we could finally see the highway. Pablo sent *El Angelito*, Luis Fernando Henao, also known as *Misil,* and Otto, so that they could check out the place of the meeting point. Indeed, José Fernando and *El Negro* Nelson were already there waiting for us. They had brought a double cab Chevrolet Luv van, a Renault 21, and a four door Toyota. Pablo and I got into the Toyota, together with *El mugre*, *El Angelito*, Otto and *El Misil*. It was driven by José Fernando. We had a radio in each car, and we turned them all on. I was always put in charge of Communications. It was one of my specialties. I studied Electronics and Communications in the Electronic and Communications Sciences Academy of Medellin. I was the best student that ever stepped into the Academy. For my thesis, I manufactured a television, sound equipment, and an AM radio. I was Valedictorian and I received a very special diploma.

We went out in the cars towards the main park of Envigado. We took a steep road, near to Poblado, beside a famous disco called *Camasuelta*. We arrived at the estate around three in the morning. It was *La Pesebrera, an estate owned by* a friend of my brother. It was one of his favorite places. He visited often. He liked estates with a stream and good views. Pablo was the first one to get out of the car. He entered the house, and the first thing he did was cut the phone line. José Fernando had brought a different mobile phone, from which we all called home again. Pablo didn't let us call our mother for safety reasons, because they likely had her phone line tapped. Besides, the idea was for me to go and greet her personally and tell her what had happened. My mother was what was most sacred to us, and we had to protect her. I took one of the cars driven by El Negro towards El Poblado.

It was sunrise. At that time, they were already sleeping in my mother's house. Her driver opened the door, and I entered her room in the second floor of the apartment. "Mom, it's me, I came to tell you we are fine." She went out and she hugged me. She's a tiny woman, bright eyed and with brown hair. I hugged her with all the force of my soul and I told her how much I love her. I wanted to express with detail, our appreciation for all the suffering she withstood for us during the past few days. She took my arm, and we went together to the hall to talk. I couldn't tell her all of the details of what had happened to us, but the important thing was to be clear that the tunnel was a fake story invented by us. She calmed down, I gave her a message from Pablo, and we talked for a while longer. I couldn't overstay because that would put her in danger and would also put in danger my freedom, which I had just achieved. I kissed her again, and I felt the warmth of her body against mine. I recognized her immense worth as my mother, and I was so grateful to have her. Through everything, she has stood by us.

She's a true example of bravery, and what it means to be courageous. She's our impetus to keep on living. "Son, I'm gonna prepare food for you, you must be hungry." I asked her not to, because Pablo would get worried if I overstayed. However, because of her insistence, I was forced to accept. It was June 23th, 1992. While she was preparing food, I leaned out through the window, and at that time the first few cars of people going to work were seen. I thought about the possibility of the Police coming there and the difficulty I would have if I needed to escape. It was practically impossible to get out of the apartment. My mother didn't take too long getting the food ready. From the prior night, she had a special dish already prepared because she was convinced that we would return home. It was marinated chicken with potatoes and rice. A typical food that my mother made. She packed it in pots covered with aluminum foil and she gave them all to me. Before going, she gave me a handwritten letter so that I could take it to my brother Pablo. I didn't want to read it, but I supposed it was a message of motherly love and encouragement to go on. She asked me to pray a lot, and before giving her a kiss, she gave me two blessings. "One is for you, and the other is for Pablo." I took the elevator and I left. Outside, in the middle of a very sunny morning, life was normal. I didn't see any policemen or members of the military.

Pablo was waiting for me, still awake. Not all the people who had escaped from La Catedral were still there. My brother had given them instructions to all hide in different places, in order to avoid any surprises. Scattered around, we would be safer. I gave him our mother's letter. We sat down in the dining room. I served everyone the food that my mother had prepared. Otto, *El Angelito*, *Popeye* and José Fernando were beside me. Pablo asked to go to his wife's house, María Victoria, to pick up some clean clothes, shoes and some personal things. We were exhausted. We ate and we went to sleep. The escape from La Catedral had finished, and now a new chapter was beginning. This time, we had to move into hiding.

THE LAST ESCAPE

The building *Los Búcaros* right in the center of Medellin, was my first hiding spot. The apartment was located on the 14th floor, it was big and very well illuminated. I had it furnished and decorated two years ago, thinking that someday I would need it. From the huge picture window of the dining room, Somma Clinic could be seen. At the rear, we could see the hill where La Catedral jail was. I stopped for a while to look at it again. Four days later, helicopters were still flying over the area looking for us. Incredibly, on the way from the Envigado house where Pablo had stayed, to this downtown apartment, nobody had seen or identified me. I travelled in the Chevrolet Luv van, the same one we used for the escape. I had no need to use wigs or dark glasses, let alone women's dresses like the military men had told the press.

I stayed there for four days. Pablo recommended to me not to go out until things calmed down a bit because the world had heard the news reports of the escape. With my brother, we made it very clear that we would only talk on the phone, and only if it was really important. He had communicated with the journalist, Juan Gossain, to try to clarify the reason of the escape and explain his point of view. Although he didn't allow the journalist to record him, my brother made it clear for our reasons of having to escape. He explained that the situation was forced on us by the Government itself, and that the President didn't want to speak with him. My brother still had the firm intention to go back to jail, he didn't care if he was transferred to a military garrison. Anywhere, except a police station. But this time, he didn't get an answer either.

In the apartment, I lived together with a lady named Nohelia, and her little five year old kid, Edwar. The little boy didn't know who I was, not even my real name, because I had changed it. I told them that I was Alberto Ramírez in the event that someone asked him about me. Just like that, I remained for four days in the apartment, and the lady cooked for me and washed my clothes. She bought my newspapers and the necessary things so that I wouldn't have to leave apartment. I had brought cash, about three million pesos, enough to survive hidden there for a long time. *El Angelito* was also with me, to whom Pablo had instructed to serve as a bodyguard to me and to run my errands. It was he who brought me the wigs, the glasses and other implements necessary for taking walks to the center of the city, because the confinement was starting to be a bit depressing.

The fifth day, I made the decision to return to the streets. I was disguised with a wig, glasses and a beard. A dark dress coat and tie gave me the look of a rabbi that had just arrived to the city. I put on a pair of leather tennis shoes, and I used a leather cover on the outside of them so that if I had to run, I could do so while the shoes matched the color of the rest of my outfit. Nobody would recognize me. I felt calm and was happy with the thought that I could walk the streets of Medellin again, especially to the center. I liked the hustle and bustle of the city, the sellers screaming, the cars, the couples kissing on the corners and the ladies looking at the glass displays. In the elevator, I got my first scare. When I opened the door, I saw a man who also had trouble with the law. We knew each other really well. He was also hiding in the same building, in the apartment next to mine. The man didn't recognize me. He greeted me and he said goodbye when he arrived on the first floor.

I was with *El Angelito*, who had also been disguised. I was carrying little Edwar in my arms. His mother, Nohelia, also went out with us. We took Oriental Avenue, and we walked searching for an ice cream store. As time and the city blocks passed by in the middle of the city, I started feeling more confident. The center of the city was going to be my best place to hide. Nobody would have ever thought that Roberto Escobar Gaviría, Pablo Escobar's older brother, would be walking down the big Avenues in Medellin while passing by the National Police Station.

We arrived to Versalles Ice Cream Shop, one of my favorites, with the idea of eating Argentinian *empanadas*. With my brother, we used to eat *empanadas* and *buñuelos* there, and I had been repressing my craving since my surrender to La Catedral. We were accommodated with a table at the back of the store, against the wall that overlooked the street. However, even though we were not recognized, we couldn't be totally careless. We talked with *El Angelito* about the elevator episode, and we concluded that if that man hadn't recognized us, it would be really difficult for somebody else to. However, *El Angelito* had a healthy amount of paranoia. "Boss, that man saw us clearly and couldn't recognize us," he told me. He then pointed out to me that there were now posters with our faces spreading everywhere, offering a reward of 500 million pesos for the recapture of any of us.

El Angelito raised my fears, and I didn't feel comfortable going back to the apartment on the 14th floor of the building anymore. We couldn't go to our relatives' houses, because the police would surely have them watched. We concluded that the best thing for us would be to go to a hotel in the center of the city, in a ghetto area where they had homes that they referred to as *shit holes*. We asked Nohelia to go to the apartment and bring us clothes, money and our personal things. Right there, in the ice cream store, we waited for her while we ate *empanadas* and *buñuelos*.

Meanwhile, I wondered if there was a way to clear up any doubts that the elevator guy had left on us. I explained to *Angelito* that the idea was to send an anonymous letter to the gentleman, in which we would let him know that police had located him and that they would drop in at any moment.

In our writing, we told him the number of the apartment where he was staying, and even the color of his car and the license plate. We were trying to give him a scare so that he would move out of the building, and then we could move back in. The truth is that I really like that apartment because it was comfortable and well located. We put the plan into practice immediately. Right there, in the ice cream store, we wrote the letter by hand, and we put it in an envelope, and we left it in the reception desk. We walked for a while after leaving the letter, and we started looking for a hotel. It had to be small and inexpensive, in order for us to go unnoticed. We found one in front of Bolívar Park, very close to the Metropolitan Church. Before going to sleep, I called Pablo on his mobile phone, and I used a pay phone. He told me he that he was getting ready to leave the current house that he was in, and that he had found a better place to hide out.

The following day, we went out early to a sporting goods store to buy some tents. We went back to the hotel, and we stayed there the whole day. We ordered food to the room, and we killed time watching movies. At night, around ten, we went out to a friend's house, who owned a motorcycle and bicycle store located very close to the hotel. The friend, José Puerta, lived within the store, which was called *Almacenes El Rin*. I knocked on the door, and he opened it himself. He didn't recognize me, and he told me that after eight in the evening, he would be closed for the day. I explained to him that I was Roberto Escobar, but he didn't believe me. "That's not you, don't talk shit," he said and he shut the door. From outside, I insisted and I talked about stories of our friendship and details times when we were cycling together. He then realized that it really was me. He opened the door, he looked at my face again, and he hugged me. He allowed us to stay overnight, and his wife got up to prepare food for us and fix the beds in a room in the back of the house, behind the workshop. The following day at six in the morning, we got ready to go out to the countryside. The day before, I had purchased a new van and some tents. They brought both early. I picked up Nohelia and her son. I asked José to lend me a few dogs, and I told him we were going hunting. I told Nohelia to drive, and to have her son sit in the front seat. *Angelito* and I sat ourselves in the rear. We the tents that we had bought into the van. The dogs were in the van too. We departed towards Bolivar City around seven o'clock, a town located about 120 kilometers away from Medellin and on the outskirts of Choco. We stopped in a restaurant beside the highway, in a place called *Bolonbono*, on the edge of the Cauca River. I ordered marinated *guagua*, a sort of big rabbit with delicious meat. The others ordered fish. We arrived later than expected, around four o'clock in the afternoon, since we had stopped a few times to admire the beautiful views. The place at which we arrived was called *Farallones del Citará*, in the lower part of the mountain with the same name, of about 3,400 meters high, famous not only because of its exotic beauty, but also because of the aircraft accidents that have occurred near its peak. History describes it as the settlement area of Citaraes and Naratupes Indians. Tourists from all around the world go there, attracted by the excellent fishing and hunting in a nice, cool climate.

As it was Monday, the beginning of the week, no tourists were to be found. *Angelito* and I were disguised, each with a wig, a pair of glasses, and our hunting gear. We setup the tents on the edge of the gorge. We prepared ham and cheese sandwiches, and everyone ate before nightfall. Nohelia and her son slept in one of the tents, and *Angelito* and I slept in the other one. We listened to the radio for a while, and we reminisced about other times when we had been on the run. The peacefulness of the night and the natural sounds from the forest made us fall asleep. The following day at seven in the morning, I sent Nohelia to buy food for the rest of the week. I warned her not to buy any meat because we were sure that with the hunting dogs and our fishing gear, we would have enough food to eat. We thought of rabbit and *guagua*, and we even believed it would be enough to bring for Pablo and the others. Nohelia stayed in the tent, while *Angelito* and I went out for an adventure. Four hours later, we came back to the tents exhausted, dying of hunger, and with no rabbit or guagua. We settled in when we saw Nohelia had set a special pot to prepare *sanchoco* over some burning firewood, and only the meat was missing. As a good Medellinean woman, she laughed before explaining that, knowing we would probably not bring any meat back to camp, she had decided to buy some beef. We had lunch after our hunting failure, and because we felt defeated we dismantled the tents and then we packed everything up so that we could return to Medellin.

Before the hunting trip, the night before, *Angelito* had gathered with some people that my brother trusted. Apparently Pablo bought and rented some apartments in different areas of Medellin, except for Envigado and El Poblado.

We arrived at a hotel in the center of the city. Before going to sleep that night, I sent Nohelia to the apartment on the 14th floor of the *Búcaros* building, so that she could check on the man to see if he was still there. Then I communicated with Pablo, and I told him that we had already bought five properties and that the guys had fixed and furnished them in order to be occupied when we needed them most. Pablo said he had done the same. My brother had already moved into an apartment. He was moving around with Otto and *Popeye*. One of the houses that we bought was located near Boston Park, also in the center of Medellin.

We left the apartment building, and we went to the house. It was a large place with two floors, very well located. It had a fountain in the backyard. A typical Antioquenian house, which are almost no longer seen. Two well-known people of Antioquenian society did us a favor so that we could buy the house. They bought the house in their name with the money that we sent them, and they lived in the house. I went there with *Angelito*. The other apartment was left intact, in case we had to go back. I bought Nohelia a beeper, and I loaned her the van. For safety, I didn't tell her where I would be moving to. I bought a Renault 4, which I was only going to use for the Antioquenian house. I reactivated the mobile phone that I had brought with me from La Catedral, and I called Pablo. We arranged a meeting time at a site, which we had talked about three days ago. It was inside the Metropolitan Church. We used a codename for the site. We called it Coltejer. We met at eight in the evening. He arrived punctual, dressed with blue jeans and tennis shoes, a green jacket, transparent shoes, a wig and Pablo had grown a really large beard. He had removed his moustache, which he had let grow in La Catedral. We were both very emotional because it was the first time that we saw each other after the escape. He was smiling and was really calm. He greeted me, shaking my hand and we went out of the church immediately. I went in my new little car, the Renault 4. He had left the other car stored in a parking garage nearby. *Popeye* and Otto went with him.

We got in the other car, and we went to the house. He really liked that house. When we arrived, I showed him *Caleto*, a very affectionate, little white dog, who had been brought by the husband who cared for the house. Despite the love he felt for animals, Pablo really didn't like having dogs or cats living with him. That night, we ate together. The lady of the house prepared a special type of lasagna for us. We talked for a while, we laughed and we remembered the La Catedral episode gratefully. The lady organized a room for Pablo in the second floor, in the main bedroom. *Popeye* and I slept in one bedroom. Otto slept in the other bedroom. For Pablo, Otto was his most trustworthy man, and maybe his most appreciated worker. He was always with Pablo. They were together through all of the good and all of the bad. Pablo went to bed late, as usual, at four in the morning. He used to say it was better to sleep during the day so that nobody would see him, and to be out during the daytime was really dangerous. Because of that, he would always wake up very late. The following day, he got up at like two in the afternoon. He wrote some letters, he read the newspapers, and he called some workers of his. He no longer talked on the phone with his family, and he forbid us all from doing the same. His preferred means of communication was writing. He wrote to everyone: his children, his wife, our mother. The letters, all of them, ended with, "Burn it after reading it!" He created a very special mailing system. He hired eleven or twelve year old boys with bikes. There were about three or four of them. He sent the letters out with some of the boys, and gave the boys the addresses and a map with locations marked out. He told them that they had to go against traffic, through the main avenues of the city. It was a sort of relay race. The first boy went to a certain address with the mail, where another one was waiting for him, who continued on the route, and this one gave it to a third boy, who went to the indicated place on the map. Alvaro, or *Limón* (*Lemon*), as we used to call him, was always waiting in the last location. He was the last link in the chain. The system was perfect and no one could follow it. The Search Units always travelled by car, which made it difficult to follow the boys against the traffic. It was an impenetrable system and made it difficult for anybody to figure out or intercept.

During the second night in our friends' house, Pablo got ready for us to go out on the streets together for the first time. He only took Otto. He wore the long curly wig, similar to the football player Leonel Alvarez's hair. It was fashionable. He put on transparent eyeglasses with round lenses, which gave him an intellectual look.

Equally, I went out in blue jeans, a long jacket, a short-haired wig, and a pair of glasses. We went out around eight at night and took Junin Avenue. We went across the entire center of the city, in the middle of all of the people while the stores were beginning to close for the evening. I took him to *Versalles* ice cream store, in which I had already been with *Angelito*. It was a famous Medellin site because it was visited by intellectuals and nadaists. Gonzalo Arango, the famous leader of this movement, used to visit it, and he would gather there for hours, making *tertulias*. During the sixties and seventies, it was the fashionable place in the city, and at night it was common to see the guys standing outside talking and eating the famous Argentinian *empanadas*. Its owner, Ricardo Nieto, was an Argentinian immigrant, who was really beloved in the city because he was also the founder of the Gardelian House. Because of that, the ice cream store was also visited by the Argentinian residents in Medellin. Julio Arrastía, the expert sports journalist, the football coach Osvaldo Zubeldía, several players of El Nacional, and the Medellin team, were among its best customers.

Pablo Escobar also joined that list, but in disguise with a wig, glasses and an all-around intellectual look. We decided to call him Doctor Echavarría, and that's how he entered the ice cream store, walking among the clients who went in and out, and talking normally to us as if he was a regular visitor to the place. We stood waiting for a table to be emptied, and we sat ourselves at the back of the saloon, facing the street. Pablo ordered a coffee with milk, three *empanadas* and a *buñuelo*. I drank soda, and I ate *empanadas*. We stayed there for about 45 minutes, and Pablo suggested that we continue the tour around the center of the city.

We entered the Caravana store, one of the most popular in the city. We bought personal items. Pablo bought underwear. Outside, in a street stall, he bought a cassette with the just released record of the history of the La Catedral escape.

We walked along Carabobo Avenue to Ayacucho Street. It was about ten at night. We passed by the National Palace, which at that time was Justice's head office, where the Medellin criminal courts operated and where they surely had a large file built around Pablo and his enterprise.

A few meters further, in front of the governor's palace, Pablo stopped and told us to wait for a while. "I'm going to show you that that if you get captured, it's because someone betrays you, someone close to you," he said.
Of the three of us who went there, the only one who smoked was Otto. Pablo never did. He asked Otto for a cigarette, and he went to where a Police agent was guarding the Palace area. "Mister, do you have a light?" Pablo asked the uniformed officer. The guy looked at him and gladly lit the cigarette. Pablo thanked him, and then he asked for the time. "It's fifteen minutes past ten, Sir," the policeman answered. Pablo walked back over to us, and we continued on our march.

He told us that several of his trustworthy men and relatives, who were killed by the authorities, died because of the betrayal of someone close to them, and not because the Police had found them. He wanted to show us that when we walked through the streets in a calm, cool, and collected mood, it would raise less suspicion. Of course, we had to take every precaution.

We came back to the house around twelve midnight. Pablo started talking to the men, and the rest of us went to sleep. The following day we had to do some shopping. This task couldn't be done by ourselves. Due to my brother's instructions, going in and out of the house had to be done carefully and with some restrictions. Everything was done by the lady or her husband. Pablo sent them to the market in the *Placita de Flores* (*Flowers Park*), one of the most traditional in Medellin. He liked it because the vegetables were fresh, and the beans were brought directly from the countryside, and they sold corn and yellow corn *arepas*, which he liked very much. The other supplies were bought in the Éxito market in San Antonio.

No doubt the hardest thing at that time was to lookout for our own personal safety. No one could know where we lived except us. Not even our families had access to that information. It was the best decision, and it guaranteed our safety and theirs. We even had guards protecting our families. It was hard not to see or speak with my mother, and it was also hard not being able to enjoy her delicious homemade food.

For Pablo, it was clear that we had to limit our outings. Except for special instances could we leave, and only with a strict set of rules. We used a fairly basic, yet quiet effective security system. For our outings, each one of us had been given a specific time that we could leave. The same went for our return. A trip could not take longer than an hour. We waited ten more minutes, in a few extreme cases. If the person didn't come back within that timeframe, we would immediately relocate to another house. Pablo was afraid someone us would get caught and be tortured until they revealed our location. The return trip of whomever left the house was always very tense. We had to walk around the house several times before entering. The police could be inside, and it was better to enter safely. From inside, there was also a monitor for whomever had just arrived, in case someone was being followed. These were very tense moments.

My brother had asked the lady of the house to invite friends to take coffee or tea in the afternoon. This made things appear more natural. The house had to look like a run-of-the-mill family house. She even kept the doors open for several hours. We were always upstairs, on the second floor. Several times, while Pablo and I wrote letters, in the first floor the husband catered to their friends, neighbors of the block for visits that lasted up to two, three or sometimes a few hours. Nobody would ever suspect that just one floor above, the most widely searched for man in the world was located. One day, we heard one of the visitors talking to our friends about Pablo Escobar's escape, and about how lucky the person who knew where to find him would be in order to claim the 500 million peso reward that the Government offered. Pablo lightly smiled, and he underscored the same thing as always, "The more natural things appear to be, the safer we are."

At night when we were lying down in bed, I used to hear Pablo recording his voice. He had bought a small sound recorder, and he used to spend hours recording messages to his children, consoling them, advising them, and asking them for patience and for them to be happy. He told them stories, and he sang songs. He did the same with his wife. Several of these dictated messages are still conserved by his little daughter Manuela.

Pablo saw that it was time find a new place to stay. It had been 20 days, and things were getting a bit risky. My brother was the first one to leave, together with Otto. I took them to the parking spot where I had left my car. Pablo drove it himself. The new house was ready, and it was also in the center of the city. Before getting in his car, Pablo told me that he would come to visit every three days during the evening. I waited up late for him, and when he arrived we had coffee prepared for him. He always drank his coffee with milk. He didn't like Colombian coffee. We played cards until late at the night, and we made bonfires in the central courtyard of the house.

One night, he didn't come to the house like he usually did. Instead he called me on the phone, and he asked me to go to one of our meeting places, which was Coltejer. In our secret code, this meant the Metropolitan Church. There, I picked up *Godoy*, a cheerful, tall, thick, dark skinned person, a very trustworthy worker for Pablo. He had helped Pablo with the escapes from Magdalena Medio. *Godoy* took me to the house where he lived with Pablo. The house was located a few meters away from the Prado Clinic, one of the best known in the city, specializing in maternity. My brother's new house had two floors, and in the lower part it had a big wooden door, which was used as a garage entrance. When we arrived, the door opened up, and we drove my car in. I noticed Pablo's car wasn't there. I got out of the car. He was waiting for me, and we went up to his room. It was a comfortable place, well-furnished and with a lot of space. "I have to tell you about an amazing story that happened to me today," he told me.

It turns out that we used to pick up the mail around seven in the evening. *Godoy* took Pablo's car, the Renault 4, to a parking garage. He stored it there so that whoever brought the mail to the house wouldn't be able to identify the car. *Godoy* received the mail a few blocks away, which was near our parking spot. The messenger was watched by messenger by another employee of Pablo. Meanwhile, neither *Godoy* nor the messenger knew that there was someone else watching them. This third person was in contact with Pablo using only a beeper. In the event of an emergency, or if he found out that someone was following *Godoy* or the messenger, he would immediately send a coded message to my brother, "Please call Grandma." If this were to happen, then Pablo already knew that there was imminent danger, and he would then have enough time to run away to a safer location. The mail delivery was made at around seven in the evening, when the streets were full of people. With thousands of people walking in all directions, any type of chase would be difficult for the police to act upon, and to distinguish people among the crowd was almost impossible. The mail operation never took more than 15 minutes. Before getting in the car to return to the house, *Godoy* had to make sure that nobody had followed him, not even the messenger, who had just given him the mail.

Pablo told me that night, when *Godoy* was coming back with the mail, he couldn't let him in immediately because he didn't hear the car horn. He was watching the evening news, which that day was delayed because of a presidential speech. When Pablo heard him, he ran out towards the garage, and he opened both doors. When *Godoy* was entering the car and my brother was holding the door, two men arrived at the house on motorbikes. They were two young guys, one of which took out a weapon. He walked up to *Godoy*'s window and he pointed a gun at his head. My brother stood still. He was carrying one of the several Sig Sauer pistols that he liked. He didn't dare to take it out, while the guy was yelling at *Godoy,* and forcing him to get out of the car. Pablo got a little closer to the car, and told *Godoy* to give them the car keys. When he heard that, the robber looked at my brother in the face, and while Pablo had expected to be recognized, the guy said, "Don't move, prick, I have enough bullets for you too!" So Pablo told *Godoy* to get out of the car quickly. The two young robbers left. One on the motorbike and the other one in Pablo's car, with the mail and everything. What hurt him the most was that the mail being stolen had been a large envelope with about fifty letters from his wife, from his children, from our mother, from his employees, from the lawyers and from his political friends.

"That's for you to see, brother, how unsafe this city has become," Pablo told me. He added that was a result of poverty, and the lack of employment. Right away he pointed out that two young men had succeeded in what thousands of soldiers and policemen had never been able to do in his entire lifetime, to intimidate him.

So the episode was a warning shot for us. Immediately, he asked me to find a new house for him to live in. Only *Godoy* and the maid remained there. We never returned to that place because sooner or later the robbers would have become aware that they had Pablo Escobar's mail in their possession. That same night we went out to the Boston house. He accompanied us there for a few days, during which we didn't go out to the streets. We remained locked inside the bedroom, and we talked until the early hours of the morning. Pablo watched the newscast, and he was on alert. The third day, my brother decided to go to another apartment. We took him by taxi. It was seven in the evening, and Pablo was disguised with a wig, a pair of glasses and a long-sleeved blue sweater. He had a longer beard now. Pablo owned the taxi. In each house that we used to hide, we had a different car which we only used for that particular location. Pablo came to own over 30 taxis, in addition to his personal cars. He used to say that travelling by taxi was safer. Each one of those cars was equipped with a radiophone, interconnected with the other cars. It was an internal communications system, which looked like the same kind of radio that the big taxi companies in the city use. We got inside the taxi in front of the Boston neighborhood house, and we went out to the center of the city. The idea was to transfer Pablo to another car, which we had already purchased. It was a blue-colored Chevrolet Sprint. They had it parked on Bolivar Avenue and Caracas Street. Pablo had to get out of the taxi into this new car, on the other side of the street. He got out and when he was crossing the avenue, a military convoy passed by us that was composed of four trucks full of soldiers, and escorted by three motorbikes. Pablo's response was not to go back to the car. He simply kept on walking, raised his hand and waived at the soldiers, who likely didn't notice him because they were passing so quickly that they had to concentrate on not falling off the sides of the trucks.

This time when Pablo left, he decided to leave the city. He departed to San Luis, a town located about 100 kilometers away, and he took the Medellin-Bogota highway. He took his wife and kids. They went deep into the hills, in a countryside house beside which there was a river which formed a pond just in front of the house. Pablo liked to bathe in the river, more than in a swimming pool. He wanted to be surrounded by nature. He felt tired and tense. It was a way for him to take a break and continue on his path to freedom. He remained there for several days before coming back to the city.

I came back to the Boston house thinking about what had just happened. Pablo was always comfortable living life on the edge, taking risks at every turn. Right now, more than ever, I believed that he was correct when he said that you get betrayed by your friends. I remembered other times in the past, from years ago, in which my brother was face to face with the police or military.

I remembered, for example, what happened to us in an estate, a few months before showing up to La Catedral. My brother was already being sought after. It happened in Amaga village, a little town in the southwest, one hour away from Medellin. Amaga was famous because it was the birthplace of an ex-president of Colombia. It was about seven in the morning, and we were both sleeping in the same room. We were only accompanied by one of my workers from Manizales, named Germán Martínez. He was fixing the garden and feeding a couple of Doberman dogs that we had there. We called them *Topolino* and *Nerón*. Germán had gone to buy milk, and he left the door open. This was done on purpose not to raise any suspicion. The estate was located on the top of a little mountain, and from there the main road could be seen. The house was surrounded by pine trees and eucalyptus. He had bought it from a pilot that flew for Avianca, who never knew who I was. My employee, Germán, showed up all of a sudden. He was accompanied by four policemen and an inspector lady. Germán entered the room looking scared, and told us that the police had arrived. They were standing in the outside corridor, and Germán had promised them coffee and bread. I got worried, and I immediately woke my brother up, who was placidly sleeping beside me. He sat on the bed. Germán explained that they came to investigate the death of a person from the night before, in the lower part of the estate, close to the main entrance. The man had been shot dead. The policemen wanted to know if we had heard the shots, and they had already asked the same question to every other neighbor in the area. The policemen remained in the outside corridor drinking coffee. I put on a light haired wig, and I went out to talk to them who, apart from the coffee with milk and the bread, had also accepted some scrambled eggs, which German prepared for them. Meanwhile, I came back to the bedroom, and I calmed my brother down, but he had already gotten dressed. He put on a green sweater, some leather sandals, a t-shirt, and a wig. He said he would go out to talk to them, and then he sat at the table and chatted with them. I took advantage of the occasion and, from the door, I called the neighbors who were outside their homes, so that they could enter our place and join the meeting. The episode ended with the neighbors and local policemen gathering, talking about how unsafe the neighborhood had become. This made us feel more at ease, because we had Pablo Escobar and the police sitting at the same table. My brother asked Germán to take down some mandarins, and to give them to our guests.

I was thinking about this story while I was going back to the Boston neighborhood house. As the one from Amaga, which I have just narrated, the face to face meetings with policemen or soldiers in the middle of an investigation were many. I must admit that while my brother's astuteness helped him to avoid sticky situations, Pablo was also quite lucky. Of course, it should be recognized that he counted on very good contacts at the highest levels of Government. Pablo had good friends in the Army and the Police, and even several colonels and generals received a monthly income from him. Now I remember General Carlos Arturo Casadiego Torrado, who became the director of the institution. My brother had met him when the official was assigned to Ibague. With regards to the story which I'm going to narrate, my brother used to give that particular general 5,000,000 pesos monthly. To the other officials, he gave money according to their rank.

The country was also in turmoil because of the recent extradition of Hernán Botero Modero, the owner of the Atlético Nacional football team. My brother had scheduled a meeting with all the leaders of

Colombian professional football to protest against this act because besides being unfair, it was completely illegal. Mr. Modero had been handed over to the USA authorities for an inexistent crime. He was accused of asset laundering. The meeting took place in *El Círculo* estate, in the upper part of El Poblado neighborhood, in Medellin. The idea was to have the meeting result in an official proposal to suspend the football championship, as a protest against the illegal extradition. Besides the teams' directors, José Santacruz Londoño, Gustavo Gaviria, Gonzalo Rodriguez Gacha, Hector Roldán, my brother Pablo and I were present. Better said, the most renowned drug dealers of the country were also present at the meeting. Everybody was looking for a solution to the extradition of Modero.

The meeting had started around eight at evening and ended at 12. The directors left around half passed midnight. Only Pablo, Ottoniel González aka *Otto,* John Jairo Arias Tascón aka *Pinina*, Carlos Mario Alzate Urquijo aka *Arete*, Mario Alberto Castaño aka *El Chopo*; and a few other trustworthy men remained in the estate. At one in the morning, a Mercedes Benz arrived at the house. A woman, who was accompanying the Mercedes driver, asked for a Doctor Hernández, and she went on further to say that she also brought a bouquet of flowers for a married couple. She claimed that she had been given that address. This caught Pablo's attention, and he ordered an employee to move himself a few meters away in the event of anything unexpectedly occurring. "If you see something strange, shoot into the air," Pablo explained to the worker, known as *Carlos Negro*. Half an hour later, we heard the shot, and we all started running. We were so scared that we fell on top of each other. We stumbled to get up. We even had to run with no shirts on. The main entrance was closed, and we had to jump the wall, which surrounded the estate. The house was surrounded by the Police.

Several shots were heard, and one of them hit the wall from which I was trying to climb over. The shot hit the wall and spread chips, one of which ended up in my face. I bled a lot and I thought that they had shot me in the head. "They've shot me, they've shot me," I shouted from above. When I got to the street, I was running to where the car was. I then recalled that I hadn't seen my brother running away with us, and naturally I got worried. Of all of us, Pablo was the one who ran the least. I was the first one to get to one of our cars. I entered the rear of the vehicle, and I rested. Through the glass, I saw Pablo arriving at the car, a little calmer. "You're going to get yourselves killed. Stop running so much!" He said that it was dangerous to run during an escape. We had the Police less than 50 meters away. We escaped because the uniformed police had entered through the wrong door. That night, the Police actually captured about eight of us, including *Arete.*

We went to a nearby house. I was bleeding and with my clothes teared to pieces. Pablo patched up the wounds on my face. My brother remained concerned about that police operation, and the precision with which they had surrounded the house made Pablo question how it all occurred. Two weeks after inquiring with his contacts about how the police raid had happened, he found out the truth. The informer was one of the participants of the meeting himself, Hector Roldán, one of the drug dealers from Cali city. After the meeting ended, Hector went to the Intercontinental Hotel in Medellin, and from there he called some high up officials in the Government, apparently with the intention of benefiting somehow. But what caught Pablo's attention the most was to find out that the operation was carried out personally and orchestrated by General Casadiego Torrado, who was supposed to be a friend. From that moment on, Pablo made the decision to take away the monthly salaries for the colonels and generals. "From now on, confirmed information means paid information," Pablo told me. Now, he only gave money to military men, who provided verified information.

Another memorable escape occurred from the famous *El Bizcocho* estate (*The Biscuit*). Pablo had named it that because of its beauty, and he built it in the shape of a bakery biscuit. The estate had a breathtaking view and location that Pablo had been searching for his entire life. It was in the upper part of El Poblado, and with a view from where you could see all of Medellin. My brother used to say that he liked to keep Medellin within the backdrop. "I keep Medellin engraved on my retina," he used to tell us.

El Bizcocho was my brother's favorite hiding place. It was very comfortable. It was a cabin built with treated pine trunks. It had two floors and a thatched roof. Inside, giant pictures of all of Pablo's favorite animals were on the walls. He used to say that these pictures made him feel like he did in Napoles, and he loved that he could still look down upon Medellin.

There he lived without any trouble for almost a year, taking every precaution imaginable. He had 30 bodyguards spread around the estate, each one of them with a powerful communications radio. It was a family gathering site. We all felt safe inside. The weekends were unforgettable, and the kids enjoyed themselves and played non-stop. Despite not having any swimming pool, the little children played down by the stream, which ran through the estate.

My brother's lawyers, the butlers of his estates, and people who managed his legal and illegal business also came up here. Pablo never had a bank account, neither in his name nor in someone else's name. All the money was handled in cash. The estate was also a meeting place for my brother Pablo with both the national and Medellinean political leaders.

El Bizcocho was quite a fortress. Pablo had built two thick walls around the house, each of which was reinforced with wire fencing and barbed wires on the top part. Between one wall and the other, there was a space of about 2 meters wide, where guard dogs moved around freely. Additionally, I had installed an alarm system, with sirens just like the ones on Police cars. Those were connected to the electric wiring, and also to some special backup batteries. If electricity was cut off, the battery system activated immediately.

After about one year of staying in that house on the Monday after Easter, the alarms were activated. It was 4:30 in the morning. The radios did not work, and their frequencies were blocked. The bodyguards weren't able to use them to notify us. My brother woke up immediately, and had five of his best armed guys ready. He used to sleep wearing blue jeans with the button and zipper undone. He put on his white Adidas shoes and waited. From a window, we could see that the military had the entire house surrounded. At six, the military decided to move in. Pablo noticed that they were mostly soldiers who had just entered the military service. In strategic places around the estate, the military had little wooden bridges made for jumping over the walls which surrounded the house without getting hurt by the barbed wires. Pablo climbed over one of the enclosures, and he walked towards a pine forest located about 300 meters away. They went out towards the west part of the city, looking for Las Palmas highway. They crossed a gorge. Pablo, a guy called Albeiro Ariza, whom we called *El Campeón*, *Popeye*, *El Chopo* and the always reliable Otoniel Gonzalez, were on foot. Pablo used to say that Otto was his lucky charm. A total of 43 people made it out of the estate, including employees and escorts. 47 of them were captured, including *Popeye*, who was injured because he was shot in the leg. The escapees reached the forest. Before getting there, a photographer of the newspaper *El Colombiano* from Medellin, appeared. The man looked at Pablo and begged him to let him take a picture. Pablo accepted, but under the condition of only publishing it after his death. The journalist accepted, and he photographed Pablo while he was on the run.

The military operation consisted of 3 large units. The last unit was placed one kilometer away from the estate, branched in a circular formation. Just as Pablo and his men thought they had avoided being captured in the siege, a little black soldier appeared. He was a tiny man, about 18 years old. Despite his skin color, he looked quite pale, and he was noticeably very nervous. His weak arms trembled, which were clearly short and extremely skinny. He almost couldn't hold the riffle, and he relied on the shoulder strap that was hanging from his left shoulder. The skinny little infantryman pointed the weapon at Pablo and his men, barely 10 meters away from them. "Hands up," he screamed. Pablo came up with one of his incredible Medellinean ideas, and calming the guy down he said, "Don't worry, we are all part of the same operation. We are with F-2." Pablo told him he was a civilian police officer, and that he had just captured one of the fugitives. He took the bodyguard whom we called Orejitas, and turned him over to the military man. "Take this one, myself and my men will keep chasing behind the others who have escaped." The soldier accepted gladly, and my brother Pablo and the others continued on the route to Las Palmas highway. The way was already cleared. Additionally, my cousin Gustavo Gaviría had located two workers in another part of the city, with the order to shoot into the air, and distract the military away from where Pablo and his men were. Two women, also hired by my cousin, handled the task of calling the radio stations and the Army Brigade, to inform them the fugitives had been seen close to the Intercontinental Hotel. Because of this, the military would end up even more confused. That made it easier to get to the Memo Pérez estate rather quickly. They stayed there until midnight. Another new escape had just begun!

I have always believed that luck has played a vital part in the life of Pablo Escobar. Not only had he escaped the military and police operations, but also seemingly ran away from death itself so many times. Pablo had a fleet of seven helicopters placed in the main airports of the country. He also had a convoy of 20 airplanes, equally spread out in different locations around Colombia. He used them for political campaigns, to visit lawyers, to transport politician friends, to go to Hacienda Napoles, and to spread money and gifts in the most obscure and forgotten about areas of the country.

In the summer of 1987, Pablo organized a trip to the Choco jungle, straight into the heart of an indigenous tribal village. Two weeks before, also by helicopter, Pablo and a group of his workers landed there in an emergency when he was coming back from bringing in cash, which was picked up weekly in Panama. My brother was travelling to Panama frequently to gather with powerful men in that country to further analyze topics related to the drug business. Many decisions were handled directly and personally, and he didn't allow any intermediaries, Not even me. That's how, while coming back to Colombian territory and being forced to land, he met the Muri Indians, who had their village on the edge of two rivers which practically crossed at a common point. That day, he was assisted by the Chief of the tribe, with whom he began an excellent relationship. The Chief told my brother that they were working on the construction of a little school, and with great effort, they were finishing the school bit by bit. Pablo asked him for a list of things they needed for construction, and the Chief joyfully accepted. They asked for pencils, pens, ink, tape, crayons, markers, paper, notebooks, books, chalk, scissors, clay, batteries, flashlights, and a whole lot of studying materials. Pablo promised he would come back in less than a month with everything that they had requested.

When he arrived in Medellin, he gave two of his men the task of buying everything that the tribe had asked for. Within a week they had gathered all of the items, and the following week he was already organizing his trip to the rainforest. He ordered two helicopters to be made ready, new twin turbine helicopter and a Hughes MD 500. In the bigger one, they loaded the boxes with all of the required items, and my brother, Otoniel and a beautiful friend who accompanied him at that time, whose name was Elsy, sat themselves in the other one. Elsy was blonde, tall and well proportioned, and had just been crowned a beauty queen. Pablo had met her in one of the many parties and popular bazaars of the little towns where he used to go on weekends. The pilot, who was the one most trusted by Pablo, was José, but he was affectionately known as *Pepe Grillo*. Both helicopters departed around ten, on a trip that took about three hours. One departed from Rionegro, and the other one, with Pablo and the others, from Envigado. The weather was perfect. Except for the threat of rain when we were flying over the Coco rainforest, the conditions were normal. The helicopters landed on a little beach, which marked the crossing of the rivers, Bagado and Murri. About 100 meters from that place, the first wooden tribal houses began. Women, elders, and children had prepared a welcome committee for us, and they formed a large lineup which looked like a thin straight line from above, marked with black ink over a giant piece of paper. They received the red carpet treatment. These tribal members wore loincloths, and the women in the tribe lived with their breasts exposed. They placed necklaces on the newcomers as a sign of welcoming, and they moved them to the main house. Meanwhile, several of the youngest and strongest of the tribe were in charge of unloading the requested gifts. The kids jumped with joy when they saw that their dream had come true. They would finally be able to finish the community school. Pablo and the tribal Chief went inside one of the houses to talk. He explained that night they would have a special ritual for the guests as a sign of gratitude. They prepared typical food from the rainforest area for them.

The main dish was roasted mountain snake with monkey and pieces of marinated anteater pulp. The main dish was served with yucca and bananas and slowly cooked coconut cream. All the food was served in pots and burnt wood dishes. Once the night fell, the ritual with their indigenous chants began. A big *totuma* pot started to move around among the guests. It was corn *chicha* heavily fermented. From the typical tribal rhythms, they rapidly moved to tropical songs. They wanted to please Pablo and the others' taste in music. Pablo danced the *mapalé,* and he made them put one of his favorite cassettes in a tape player. It was the Russian song, *chachacha*. They all danced. Otto liked the teacher from the little school, and he asked her to dance. Both looked like they were having a good time, but that wasn't well received by the Chief. Pablo, when noticing this, offered his new friend, the queen, to accompany the chief in the following music round, as a sign of friendship. That smoothed things over, and the party continued until after two in the morning. During the following three days, the group devoted time to hunting and fishing. Pablo had brought the necessary items for one of his favorite hobbies, including hunting rifles, fishhooks, and camping equipment. Accompanied by two guides, they went deep into the rainforest. Before every helicopter trip, Pablo prepared a plastic jar filled with matches for starting a campfire. He said that, in the event of an emergency landing, it would be good to have these on hand. A campfire, according to him, could become our best friend at night, while the smoke was an excellent means of communication in the middle of a rainforest like Choco. After four days and with the mission accomplished, Pablo ordered the return trip to Medellin. Otto insisted on bringing the indigenous teacher to the city, but both Pablo and the tribal Chief convinced him to give up on this idea, because besides being forbidden for them to leave the rainforest, it could be misunderstood as being disrespectful on behalf of Pablo. At one in the afternoon, Pablo decided at the last minute to change helicopters. He would rather make the return trip in the Huey. It was piloted by an experienced air man, an ex-Government official, whose last name was Carvajal. Otto sat in the front, while Pablo and the beauty queen sat in the rear. Despite the persistent drizzle that was coming down, the captain explained that the general conditions for the entire flight would be pretty normal. Everything went perfectly well, even when the first Envigado houses started to be seen from Pablo's window. The other helicopter was in front. The Huey started to prepare its descent toward the house where Pablo was planning to stay, and where his bodyguards were waiting in two cars. At around 7,000 meters, the helicopter began to shake at intervals of about ten to fifteen seconds. The flight indicators weren't showing anything, even when the pilot felt that he had lost control. It was clearly the tail rotor malfunctioning. The system that brought stability to the helicopter, had broken down. They were now a few seconds away from certain death. The captain was losing his cool, and he managed to have enough time to turn on the radio and notify the pilot of the other helicopter. "We're losing altitude. We're going down. We're going to die. Oh my god. We're going to die!" Captain Carvajal screamed. The queen broke down in tears. Pablo held the handle tight, leaned down his head, casted a blessing and entrusted his life to the Virgin. Despite everybody else's fears, he never showed any signs of despair. He was always calm, even in the most intense moments of his life. "Tranquility is the best guide, because it allows you think clearly during the worst moments," he used to tell us. The helicopter was going down. First, it crashed into some high pine trees in a paddock, then it ended up on a cliff. They were lucky to fall over a swampy area, which acted as a natural cushion that had eased the impact of the crash. The helicopter fell headfirst into the swamp, and it ended up with the tail pointing upwards. It didn't catch on fire. Pablo climbed out first, a little scraped and scatterbrained, but in good condition. He helped the young queen out of the helicopter, who was crying out loud, helping to raise intrigue among the neighbors who were already starting to reach the crash site. The pilot was also alive. Nobody died. Otto reached the exit, and he held Pablo's arm at once, and made him move away from the crash. The other helicopter had already landed, and the crew ran towards the crash site. The beauty queen remained lying on the cliff, with her arm broken, and some people helped her to get to the hospital. The pilot was crying and really shaken, and Pablo recommended to him that he stay there for a while and wait for the authorities to arrive. My brother and Otto went up to the other helicopter, which was waiting with the motors on, ready to take off again. Once he reached the first few meters of altitude, Pablo took a suitcase that was beside his seat. He unlatched the guard plates, and he opened the window; dropping thousands and thousands of banknotes over the people who had gathered at the crash site. He always carried huge sums of money as a precaution. From above, the police cars could be seen heading toward the crash. Everyone, cops, neighbors, and curious people had arrived at the scene of the accident, were all now focused on running desperately after the flying banknotes that rained from the sky like a gift from God. No one knew that the man, who had been saved by a pure miracle, was Pablo Escobar himself. The story was reported as a normal accident of a helicopter flight that was properly authorized by the Civil Aeronautics Administration. Pablo promised that he would build a big altar there for the Virgin who had just saved him. He said it was a real miracle, of those which our mother always talked about. This time, the miracle helped him to escape from the hands of death. "The Holy Virgin saved us," he claimed.

Everyone remembers the La Catedral escape. I think my brother and I were involved in even more spectacular getaways. There was one which was heavily publicized, the one from *El Loro*. *El Loro* was an estate located on the edge of the Cocorná River, about 10 kilometers above the Magdalena River. I had sent José Fernando Posada Fierro to buy me some livestock in the Berrio Port. When he was arriving at the village, he saw a fleet of about ten helicopters passing by, which were going towards the estate. He called my brother at El Loro and told him and his workers. Pablo didn't give any significance to that, and he simply told him not to worry. "No one dies this evening," he answered. He felt safe at that place, and he asked us not to worry. Gonzalo Rodríguez Gacha aka El Mexicano, Jorge Luis Ochoa and his wife were with us. Pablo had installed communication radios in a triangular formation near the estate, which would notify him in advance of any aircraft. When the helicopters passed by over Santuario, Antioquia, my brother was notified. The same happened when they arrived to San Luis, or Danta, and Pablo always said the same thing, "Keep calm. We have about two hours before they arrive here. He went to sleep, but I remained uneasy. El Mmexicano left because he had a date in Doradal. About an hour later, they gave us a new report, and I was now really worried. I woke him up and I said, "Get up, brother! Seven helicopters, some trucks, and elite motorbikes are coming." He looked at me and then asked me where they were coming from, and I explained it was from San Luis. So he said they would still take a while, and he would sleep a little longer. It was about eight in the morning.

I was worried, and I decided to change my white clothes for something more lightweight and casual. Jorge Ochoa and the others did the same. I ordered the men to saddle up some mules, we had breakfast, and I prepared some bags with food. I insisted that Pablo do the same. When I told him that they were really close, he stood up. He got his clothes ready, and when we were going to leave we saw the first commandos arriving. A massive shoot-out erupted. Pablo had installed some pointed spears into the ground on the flat side of the estate, which prevented the helicopters, which contained more troops, from landing. The helicopters were shooting at us from above, and they hit my brother-in-law, Mario Henao, who decided to not stay in the house. Mario ran down the stairs and out of the house, and then jumped into the river instead. He died instantly. We were surrounded on all sides, and we were going to be captured. All of us were armed. Pablo, *El Mexicano*, and Jorge Luis had previously performed some sort of blood covenant for situations like this. "If they capture us to give us to the gringos, we'd rather be dead," the three of them had said. It was suicide over capture. He honored the famous phrase of *Los Extraditables* (*The*

Extraditables) which warned that, "*We prefer a grave in Colombia than a jail in the USA.*" In the most critical and intense moment of that battle, Jorge Luis took a 38-caliber pistol which he carried on his waist, willing to kill himself, but Pablo didn't let him. Pablo said there was still hope, and that it wasn't yet time to die. Anyway, he frequently commented that if he ever put that plan into practice, he would shoot himself in the head. "That's certain death, and it won't fail," he used to repeat when he brought up this topic.

We managed to escape from that situation. We reached the mountain, and we hid in a cave for a while. That night, beside a river, we took a bath and we ate a little. Jorge Luis was really nervous and was persistently harassing Pablo. Later, we arrived at a friends' house and we called to be picked up. Fourteen of our workers fell during that battle with Police in the estate. Among them, a beautiful young lady who played on the Antioquian Volleyball Team. This young lady was later freed, and then a few days after that she was found dead in Medellin.

Another well-known escape occurred in the USA. We had organized a tour to Miami, Disney, Texas, Tennessee and Washington. We went with our entire family. This was before the US Government was going after Pablo, however he was already a well-known drug trafficker. One night, in Miami, all of the men went to a club named *Folice*, where a rather fat woman with a very sexy voice was singing. Her name was *Anny*, and with her melodious voice several of the men in our group got drunk. Friends of ours, whose last name was Builes, were with us. They had an Aero Van truck. One of the friends went to sleep in the van. When we all returned to the vehicle to go to the hotel, the young man had fallen asleep in the driver's seat, he woke up in a sleep-walking state, and he turned the van on and accelerated without knowing. The van hit some cars which were in front of him, and he damaged the fence to the entrance to the disco. All at once, we got out of the truck and started running. Pablo, a brother-in-law of ours, Gustavo Gaviría, *Piriña* and I were there. *Piriña* was a guy whom Pablo loved very much, and he took him on these trips, and he helped Pablo with the luggage and with our mother's errands. His name was John Jairo Arias Tascón. We ran down a street, and after running for about ten blocks, three police cars were there and they stopped us. We were all searched with our legs spread open while we were up against a wall. I was carrying $50,000 dollars cash in the case of a little photo camera, but luckily they didn't find that. They made us get in the police vehicles, and they put us in the rear. They left us there while they were responding to another incident. The officer, who was driving the patrol car, was injured and used a cane. He got out of the car, and went to a liquor store to arrest some other people. He closed the patrol car, but left it with the air conditioner on. I saw the uniformed officer's cane in the front of the car, and Pablo and I with our fingers managed to lift the stick between the bars of the interior of the car. Almost with our fingertips, we used the stick to hit the electronic door lock, which opened the door. In seconds, we reached the street, and we ran to find a taxi which took us to the hotel. As we hadn't been interrogated, nobody searched for us later. The next day, we departed to Washington, D.C.

Pablo wanted to see the FBI museum. We all went to visit it, and my brother was impressed by all of the things that they had on display: daggers, tobacco shaped pistols, one shot rifles, machines used for cheating in casinos, marked poker cards. In a nutshell, they even had clothes from Al Capone and other Italian Mafiosos. Pablo never really admiration for Al Capone, although a few days later on that same trip we went to visit a home-museum of another Mafioso. The only mobster that Pablo used to admire was Vito Corleone. "He's the real godfather," my brother used to say that with a bit of sarcasm.

We also visited the White House, we walked around it, and we entered with a Spanish speaking guide. We took a lot of photographs there with the official guards.

Later we went to a Picasso museum. Pablo liked the paintings very much, and he even bought a Picasso painting with a depiction of some bulls.

In another instance, I had to make an escape of my own from the hands of the Rionegro Police. This would happen years later. They kidnapped me in two Police patrols, and the agents asked me for a 500 million peso ransom to set me free. They knew that I was Pablo's brother. I told them not to mess with Pablo, and that he would become aware of this sooner or later. I told them that they should let me go, and I wouldn't tell anyone about what had happened. But they didn't accept, and they put me in an abandoned home with a dark fence that was close to El Peñón. There, I convinced them to let me call my brother so that he could pay the ransom money for me. I called Pablo from a pay phone, in front of the officers. "Put me on the phone with the officer," Pablo told me. I put him through and he warned him, "Don't let anything happen to my brother because when you mess with me you're in real serious trouble," he said. Pablo promised to have the cash ready, and sent a guy to pick it up and deliver the money to them. However, time passed by and nothing happened. I told them to let us move to a more populated location and my captors accepted. There, I asked them to let me call my brother again, and they accepted without a problem. I called and no one answered. I was sure I was going to be killed. It was two in the morning. I told them to turn the car on to go to the drop-off point where Pablo's guy with the money was supposed to be. That's when I took my opportunity to run. I dove into the river and they shot at me, but I was now protected by the darkness of the night. Miraculously, I was unharmed. I continued moving across the river, dying from exhaustion. I had managed to escape.

The escapes and the getaways that we had to deal with over the years were always either related to the business, or because I was Pablo Escobar's brother. However, the stronger the police or military force was, the less danger we were in. After the La Catedral escape, we thought we were going to live through the most difficult days of our lives, but that wasn't so. Except for the episode of the armed robbery to steal my brother Pablo's car, we never really felt that we were in danger of dying or falling into the hands of the authorities. Of course, the system consisted of having several clandestine safe houses. This was the best way to hide. With Pablo, we sometimes hid in the slum areas of the poorest neighborhoods of Medellin. We did this when we felt that we were taking a lot of heat. I was disguised as a construction worker, and I took the bus to travel to the upper parts of the city. A man took care of us at night, and his little kid brought us something to eat. Pablo got a bit tired of this situation and of that of our mother, our children, and our sisters. It's like we had fallen from grace. The Escobar Gaviria Family was like a wandering Jewish clan with the constant threat of persecution. Wherever the Jews went, with proper legal documents and with the intention of seeking refuge from death threats, they were seemingly always expelled without compassion. Gatherings with our mother became impossible. For her safety, when we managed to pick her up, without the Search Block agents knowing, we had to give her a pair of glasses with the lenses painted in black, so that she never knew where we were hiding. We used to transport our sisters in a bakery van painted with advertisements all around. They took them to a safe garage, and there my brother and I waited for them. We could only meet for up to 20 or 30 minutes at a time. The heat from the authorities was getting more and more intense. Now there were DEA people spread all around Colombia, and in the news they talked about the most sophisticated techniques that were being used in our search.

Pablo and I kept staying in the center of the city, in different houses. One night, he called me, and he said that I have a meeting in another Envigado house. The codename for that house was *La Maestra* (*The Teacher*), because it was really close to La Paz neighborhood, where my brother and I were raised and where my mother was both the director and a teacher in the school. I left in my blue Sprint car, accompanied by *El Angelito*. I drove through the city from north to south and on the main avenue which goes to El Poblado. The block before passing by Envigado Park, I took the road which goes to the Sabaneta district. I took the first entrance on the left side, through a site called *El Señorial*. About four hundred meters from there, in the upper part, there was the estate house, in which Pablo was waiting for me. Popeye and Otto also arrived. *El Angelito* came back to pick up my mom in El Poblado, and half an hour later she was with us. We ate and we notified my mother that we were going to surrender. "We're telling you now so that you do not get scared when we actually surrender, and we don't want you to learn about this from the news," Pablo told her. He explained it was the best thing to do in order to avoid persecution of the entire family, and she would be able to visit us without any further trouble, and without having to always meet in secret. Pablo's idea was that, after I surrendered, I would be in charge of managing and negotiating the situation with the Government. "I am also willing to surrender, mom," Pablo told her. I further explained that in the jail, I would find it easier to speak with the authorities to negotiate my brother's second voluntary surrender. We arranged for my surrender to occur in two days, while I organized my things, and made sure that all of our safe houses were ready so that Pablo could use them if he needed to. Those locations were only known by my brother. Popeye, who was listening carefully, told Pablo that he also wanted to surrender. Otto suggested doing so as well. Pablo authorized them. We set the date of my surrender for October 2nd. This meant that September 30th and October 1st, 1992, were the last two days that I would spend with my brother in person. Without knowing so, we were sharing our last few hours together, after a whole lifetime of being practically inseparable. We were like twins, despite our age difference. We loved each other very much, and we learned to grow up, to develop as youngsters and deal with adult life together. We were always there for each other, through the good and the bad; the decadence and the poverty. Those last two days became permanently ingrained in my mind. We were always alone during those final hours. We visited the homes that Pablo would stay in if needed, and I introduced to him Mr. Socorro and his wife, who were going to accompany him. I recommended the lady because she was a good cook, and because the house was quite tranquil. They look like the perfect married couple.

The day of my second surrender, I got up early, and I woke him up as per his instructions. We read the newspaper, and we listened to the news radio. We ate breakfast together. Mrs. Socorro prepared coffee with milk, scrambled eggs with onion and tomato, yellow corn *arepa*, the same ones that we bought in Flores Park. At nine in that morning, it was time for me to leave for my surrender. Pablo sent, via beeper, a message to Otto and Popeye, who had stayed together in another location. The three of us had already arranged the meeting time and place. My brother accompanied me up to the garage door. I got out of the car, I centered myself, and I said goodbye to him. He went out to the driveway. I gave him the electronic control of the garage, and I hugged him. He held me tightly, and he assured me that things would end up well. He promised me that we would see each other again soon. He was definitely going to surrender again. I walked up to the trunk of the car, and I stored two mobile phones from the Public Enterprises of Medellin. Before getting in, I looked into his eyes and I felt how much I was going to miss him. I hugged him again. Without knowing that it was the last time I would feel him beside me. It was the last hug, the goodbye hug. I started the car to go to Itaguí, up to a site where Popeye and Otto were waiting for me. We went down through Colombia Street, passing by Berrio Park, in the very center of the city. The three of us came disguised with long wigs and glasses. At the traffic light, where Colombia Street and Berrio Park crossed, while we were waiting for the lights to change, two motorcyclists parked beside us on each side. The man located in the right side of the car put his hand over the bonnet. Popeye got nervous. Neither of them was armed. When the lights changed, the man on the motorbike asked for my permission to turn left in front of me. We all sighed because we thought we would get captured before arriving at the meeting point with the Attorney. We were supposed to arrive at a furniture store, beside the main avenue. In order to get there, it was necessary to drive through the entire city. We had set an appointment with the Attorney, which was now one kilometer ahead. As a precaution. We had told them on the phone that the idea was to surrender in La Pintada, a retired population about 70 kilometers away from there. We arrived at the store. There was a lady attending to customers, and she had two young ladies with her. I told the woman, who was in charge not to worry. "We didn't come to buy furniture. My name is Roberto de Jesus Escobar Gaviria," I said. She didn't believe me, and she asked me not to hurt them. So we took off our glasses and wigs, and one of the ladies recognized me, because I was a frequent client of that store. I explained that we were going to be there for only about 10 minutes. I asked her for only one favor, "Don't answer the phone, and don't make phone calls." I did this for safety because the Government offered millions of pesos as a reward for the three of us. The three ladies were clearly very nervous. I hugged them to calm them down, and I asked for a little coffee. "Don't worry, my brother Pablo is also coming here. He is also going to surrender." We all laughed. A little bit later, the Attorney, whom we had hired to make the arrangements, had arrived. Her name is Magdalena, who is also a cousin of mine, the son of one of my mother's sisters. I asked her the favor of bringing a reporter. It was Marcela Duran, a young reporter of a television newscast in Bogota, to whom we decided to give the exclusive scoop because of her persistence and her peculiar way of contacting me. Every night she sent us messages, and she spoke on a radio station that she knew my brother and I listened to. Because of that, I got in touch with her, and I wanted her to be present. It was also a good way to make things seem more transparent with both the authorities and the nation. We told the reporter that we were going to La Pintada. I suggested to her that she wear tennis shoes and blue jeans for the trip. She looked a bit nervous when she saw us.

My cousin also accompanied the attorney, her legal team, and the reporter. Within ten minutes, we left the store. In one group, there was a guy that we called, *Pantera*, who was in charge of managing the re-surrender with the Government. We left in an armored car driven by *Pantera*, and we headed towards the Itagui penitentiary. Before leaving, we allowed the reporter to record a brief interview and inquire about the reason for our re-surrender. Popeye got upset because she called him by his nickname, and he corrected and gave her his real name, Jhon Jairo Velásquez. We entered the jail, and I was carrying sound equipment, and I had a mobile phone hidden inside of it. Nobody else knew about the phone, and I used it to help in arranging for my brother Pablo's re-surrender.

A few days later, the others followed suit and began surrendering too. My brother insisted that his intentions were firm. Everything was ready for the re-surrender. The only condition he put was that the two yards of the Penitentiary were not divided by a big thick concrete wall. He asked the Penitentiary to knock down the wall, and to let there be only one yard for everyone. The pavilions were very small. Pablo wanted enough space in the yard so that he could build a small football field. But time went by and the attorney on duty, Gustavo De Greiff, didn't offer any solutions. Pablo told me on the phone one night that he believed Attorney De Greiff's intention was to lock him up all alone in a yard, isolated from everybody. "I won't let them lock me away in isolation like this," he warned me. A few days later, unexpectedly, I was locked in yard number two. They isolated me, for a period of about ten days. They didn't let me out of my room, and I was communicating with my lawyers through an intercom in a small cubicle. I declared myself on hunger strike. I wasn't receiving sunlight. I called the Attorney and Human Rights groups, because I hadn't committed any infringement. I got them to open the door, and let me out to get some sun. Two days later, I got them to take two prisoners to my yard, Juan de Dios Urquijo and *El Gordo* (*The Fat Guy*). Pablo knew what the Attorney De Greiff's intentions towards him were, and he told me that he was no longer going to surrender.

I was worried about my brother's decision so I decided to contact Attorney De Greiff personally. He accepted the invitation for a meeting, and he came to visit me. We talked about Pablo's potential surrender, about the wall, and about the legal situation surrounding some of my brother's workers. Pablo was really worried about *La Kika*'s situation, who was Dandenis Muñoz Mosquera, one of his workers. He had been accused of putting a bomb inside an Avianca plane, and Pablo wanted to help him. At that time, Attorney De Greiff had sent a notification to the American authorities with evidence that could implicate *La Kika*. Pablo decided to contact De Greiff personally, to propose that he reconsider *La Kika's* case. He sent one of his most trusted lawyers from Medellin, Doctor Salomón Lozano. Doctor Lozano, a criminal lawyer, was received by De Greiff in his office on 35th Street and Fourth Avenue in Bogota, beside a National Park. My brother's idea was that the attorney general send a new letter to the US Prosecutors with a new version of *La Kika's* story. Pablo had Doctor Lozano send De Greiff a letter with precise instructions. "The Attorney General must read it and give it back," Pablo had told Doctor Lozano. "When he gives it back to you, burn it in front of him," he explained. Doctor Salomón Lozano talked about the case to *La Kika* and continued with the delivery of the secret message. The attorney read it. The meeting was on the fourth floor of the building, where De Greiff had his office. The Attorney was a strange man. He came across to people as being good-natured, and he aroused immediate affection in people. His popularity was very high in the country. He was considered the best anti-corruption attorney that Colombia had ever had, with an honest approach and a firm grip on prosecuting gangsters. "Let the corrupt tremble," he once came to say. This was a phrase that would change both Colombia and the world. Gustavo De Greiff, a clumsy person who used thick corrective glasses, and an inseparable pipe, went down in the history of Colombia as the first Attorney General of the Republic, after the new Constitution of 1991. But in spite of his quite famous and honest approach, Pablo didn't trust him. Pablo had a hidden ace up in his sleeve. At the 21st Notary of Bogota, behind Notary Jaime Cortés Castro, De Greiff himself had signed a document as partner and president of El Dorado Airlines and a major shareholder was no less than Gilberto Rodríguez Orejuela. If this document was disclosed, it would cost De Greiff his position as Attorney General of Colombia because it represented an insurmountable moral impediment. Because of this, the order was to burn Doctor Lozano's letter once it was read by the Attorney General. De Greiff read it with surprising astonishment, again and again, and returned it to the lawyer who was waiting impatiently. In the letter according to what Pablo would tell me days later over the phone, my brother offered Attorney De Greiff $500,000 dollars for sending a letter to the American judge who was presiding over *La Kika's* case. A few days later, Attorney General Gustavo De Greiff made public his new position about *La Kika*'s case and he sent a letter with the new evidence, which exonerated *La Kika* from any responsibility in the Avianca terrorist attack. My understanding is that the US immediately cancelled De Greiff's visa because of this incident with *La Kika*. A judicial level political storm exploded, which shook the foundation of diplomacy because the letter was not well received by US prosecutors, then headed by US Attorney General Attorney, Janet Reno. De Greiff complied with Pablo's wishes, and Pablo fulfilled his end of the bargain. A few days later, he sent the money in two leather suitcases, which Doctor Salomón Lozano himself took to Bogota. This time, the appointment wasn't in the general attorney's office, but in an apartment. I think De Greiff's sudden change of attitude raised immediate suspicion in the USA. As time went by, a DEA agent visited me in jail so that I would say that I had known about this deal with Attorney De Greiff, but I refused. I soon learned that the same inquest by the DEA was also done to Doctor Diego Londoño Withe, an old ally of my brother. He also said that he didn't know about any deal.

Our relationship with Mr. De Greiff was better than ever. My brother always said he was a, "deceitful man." He repeated again that, "Whenever somebody offers him money, he accepts it." According to Pablo, De Greiff worked for the highest bidder. Pablo was always sure that the letters he used to send to President Gaviria, and which he thought he was sending through De Greiff, never actually reached Gaviria. Perhaps the reasons for Pablos letters had been misrepresented to Gaviria. In those letters, my brother set the ground rules for his re-surrender. If Gaviria had known the rules that my brother proposed, he would surely have accepted. But Gaviria did not. Everything seemed to indicate that De Greiff used to handle them as he pleased and never actually delivered the letters. That was what frustrated my brother the most with regards to his re-surrender. President Gaviria was likely tricked by De Greiff. If things had gone as expected, Pablo would be in jail but alive. Doctor De Greiff would contact me again the day that Pablo died. He called me at my jail from his office in Bogota. "I am very sorry about your brother," he told me trying to comfort the deep sorrow which overwhelmed me. "I would have wanted to talk with him further about the many things that the authorities and Justices accused him of," he said. "I know that Pablo did not do all of the bad things that people say he did," he told me before saying goodbye. I thanked him for the kind and compassionate words, which were worthless to me at that time.

My first Christmas in that jail was really difficult. Very different than the one in La Catedral. Without my brother, who was running away, without any family, without any visits from anybody. The situation was really different. We couldn't call, they opened the mail before giving it to us, and the treatment was different. On December eighth, the lighting day, we spent the day together in the same yard. From the yard we launched balloons with five thousand peso banknotes and a written message that said "Hooray for Cartel de Medellin! Hooray for Pablo Escobar!" When the prison found out, they punished us, and we were again isolated from each other. We were moved from that yard, and they sent us to isolation cells. On Christmas day, they let us call our families before eating. We went to sleep early, and New Year's Eve followed the same protocol. The New Year started with the hope of being able to study. The legal adviser of the jail, Doctor Hilduara, was going to be our Law teacher. We all took classes, which would help with our eventual sentence reductions. We were also allowed to work in the jail's workshop, and we learned how to carve wood.

THE LETTER BOMB ATTACK

From that jail, I have two of the harshest memories of my life. The news about my brother's death, and the letter bomb attack of which I was the victim. It was Saturday, December 18th, 1993. I was at

Mass, the same way that I spent every Saturday morning. We were all very sad, and we recalled stories about Pablo. The Mass was presided by the Bellavista jail chaplain. Once the ceremony had ended, the father called me aside to comfort me. He further went on to explain that the day Pablo died he had bought a raffle ticket for a motorbike, and he had asked my brother to help him win it. "I won that bike, Roberto. Thanks to my faith in your brother," the little father told me. We were having that discussion when one of the guards called me to the other side of the room to give me the mail that had just arrived. I said goodbye to the priest, and I passed through to the other corridor. It was a large manila envelope, which an INPEC lieutenant had left for me on the table of a small cubicle. I never used to open the envelopes personally, for safety. I used to pay another guy to do it. But on that day, I wasn't the same. I entered the small two-by-two meter cubicle, and I sat beside the lieutenant to sign the mail book, which we always signed when we received mail. As this was a manila envelope with a big stamp, it didn't raise any suspicion in the jail. Additionally, I was waiting for copies of court documents, which I had asked for about eight days ago. I thought this package was a response. The package felt heavy, and I held it with both hands. I opened it through a corner of the envelope, and I saw a weird green color in its interior, which immediately made me hesitate. I stood up, and I held the package with my right hand to take off its inside enclosure. Then I noticed a little wire that poked out of a bag, and I immediate knew that it was a bomb. I didn't have time to do anything. I wanted to run to the door, and throw it into the yard, but it was already too late. It exploded, and blew me off of my feet, along with the chairs and both guards. It lifted me up to the roof, and it felt like I had broken the roof with my head. I fell on the floor almost like in slow motion. "Oh my God, don't let me die. Help me, spirits of the purgatory," I silently prayed. I saw clouds of all colors, very pretty lights surrounding me and with my left hand I touched the floor, which was wet maybe because of my blood. From the colored lights, it had now transitioned into total darkness. I couldn't see anything, I smelled like blood, and my face was bathed in it. My right hand was destroyed. No one came to my rescue. There was also blood coming out of my stomach, and I decided to crawl to the entrance. I moved as fast as I could to the door, which separated the courtyard from the corridor where the Mass was being held. I honestly didn't know if I was dead or alive, or if it was just a horrible nightmare. I screamed, and I asked for help. I arrived at a washbasin, and I washed my face. It burned like hell and I screamed again. "A bomb, a bomb, they killed me, they killed me!" I screamed in agony. The door which lead to the other corridor was electronic, and I heard the guys on the other side screaming my name. The explosion had destroyed the electronic locking system that opened the doors, and no one was coming to help me. Just like that, I lasted about 20 minutes. I calmed down. I prayed, and again I had a strange sensation of infinite tranquility come over me. "I am already dying," I thought. I have always asked God for my death be painless. I let myself become overwhelmed by the sensation of sudden tranquility, and that's when the guys came in. I was lying on the floor. I asked for a mattress and a pillow, and they immediately brought both. They laid me down, and I asked for water. I felt a sudden, unexpected thirst. I drank water and I breathed deeply. I asked for a mirror, but I couldn't see myself. I was blind, and bit by bit I was losing my sense of hearing. Several men lifted me, and they took me to the director's office. There they left me for about three inexplicably long hours. I prayed for them to take me quickly to a clinic. Maybe because of the tedious jail procedures. At last, they came for me, and they took me to Las Vegas Clinic in Medellin.

Before arriving, I lost consciousness. I had lost a lot of blood. The doctors operated on me and miraculously stabilized my condition. In the recovery room, my mother arrived first, then my sisters, cousins, and later my wife Claudia. I didn't want anyone to see me like I was. I told them to go home, because it was also dangerous and something might happen to them beside me. But Mom didn't want to. "If we die, we all die. We're not moving from here," she said emphatic. My wife, who was pregnant with my first daughter, also didn't want to abandon me. My sisters also stayed. A doctor entered with bad news. The eyes were destroyed, and they had to be removed. All I could see, was paint. It was a strange experience that brought me back to my childhood. I remember mixing paint, to create colors. My mind had stopped creating colors through my eyes, and instead my brain was creating this life. Life of colors. My family, they all cried, but at the same time said they couldn't allow that to happen. "You have to do something! We will not allow you to take his eyes away!" My wife screamed. So the doctor recommended that I should be transferred to the Bogota Military Hospital, where the experts were. My wife made no delay in hiring a private plane, and two hours later I was already at the Military Hospital. The INPEC collaborated with us and, this time they expedited their procedures. In Bogota, I was received by Doctor Hugo Pérez Villareal, an extraordinary man, warm and extremely patient, and above all an extraordinary doctor. He was considered one of the best ophthalmologists in the country. Immediately, he scheduled me for surgery. It was the night of December 20th, and I was in the operating room in the middle of a whole bunch of experts dressed in green, who murmured nonstop. The operation lasted about 10 hours. Outside, my wife was waiting impatiently. Doctor Pérez Villareal went to comfort her after my surgery, and he explained that she shouldn't worry about my eyes, and that they weren't going to take them away. "I never take my patients' eyes away, and we're going to do everything that we can to make sure that this is not the first time that we lose a set of eyes in my operating room," he told her. Claudia cried, and we now had a glimmer of hope. From that moment, Claudia was my main source of support. She was, for me, the eyes I didn't have. She stayed beside me, she pampered me she calmed me down, and she gave me love. She's a beautiful slim woman, of natural Guajirian beauty, full of patience, and with an enormous and caring heart. I owe part of my recovery to her, thanks to her tenacity and courage, thanks to her loving energy and tremendous spirit that she put into everything that she did. She helped me to want to keep moving forward with my recovery. My mother was like the lightning rod who protected me from everything. Her tiny hands, warm and now seasoned in her older years, were my encouragement in the dark, and a support system that I could rely on. Her eternal love helped me to move out of the darkness, and because of her encouragement I decided to keep on living.

In addition to my sight, I lost part of my hearing, where they have performed six surgeries. I can say with certain pride and sarcasm that I am the Colombian *Bionic Man*. The nerves in my eyes and some parts of my ear have been replaced by tiny cables, and several tissues were literally made by hand; out of fiber and wire. I stayed in the Military Hospital for a month. I was totally paranoid, and I couldn't eat anything. I didn't want to die, and I was afraid of them poisoning my food. They would not allow my family to bring me food from home, and I was always guarded by soldiers. I was getting dehydrated. I wouldn't eat or drink anything, and the doctor said that I would enter a coma at any moment. My wife became desperate, and she volunteered to try the food before I did. It was the only way for me to get back to eating peacefully. "If we die, the three of us die." Claudia told me, rubbing her stomach with the baby inside. They took me again to Medellin, to the Itagui jail. Two months later, they gave me my first cornea transplant. I was delicate in my recovery state, but they took me back to the Itagui jail anyway. I couldn't even cough, because the smallest effort could potentially damage the operation. Then I was taken to the Military Hospital again. Doctor Pérez complied with his promise. He didn't take my eyes away, and I held onto the hope of having my complete eyesight back and regaining my hearing. The therapies have also been very important in my recovery. To do this, I counted on the company of my son, José Roberto, who everyday took on the role of walking with me and acting like both my guide and my physician. José Roberto would die months later in an absurd act of violence in Medellin without ever fulfilling his big dream, running in the streets and playing football with me. The experts told me that the best doctors in the world, who specialized in advanced eye and ear procedures, were all in the USA and Europe. While I was allowed to take those trips, I'm still having my operations performed in Colombia by Doctor Pérez's blessed hands, who after 20 years have given me hope to see the colors of Antioquia and my country again.

PABLO, POLITICS AND THE PRESIDENTS

Pablo used to call Mr. Montesinos, *Montecristo*. We all called him that when we referred to him. In the middle of everything, he turned out to be a pleasant guy. In Hacienda Napoles, he had fun more than ever. Pablo had a very special gift for his first night after dinner beside the swimming pool. Through a friend of his in Brazil, he had five beautiful *garotas* flown in from Rio de Janeiro, which is what they call beautiful young women in that country. There were ladies for all tastes: dark haired, brown haired, blonde, tall, short, all of them voluptuous and attractive. Their Brazilian charms became quite clear due to the look of awe that Montesinos exhibited on his face. Our illustrious visitor sat with his eyes wide open while observing the movements of the dancers who circled his vision. It was a gift that Pablo knew would please his guest, because we had been told by the Peruvians about Montesinos' love of beautiful women. The next day, an equally unforgettable experience was waiting for Montesinos in the Hacienda. He got up early, and he had a typical Medellinean dish for breakfast, with *arepas* brought from Medellin, scrambled eggs with rice and hot coffee with fresh milk just taken from the cow. My brother took Montesinos to accompany him on one of his favorite pleasures. On 4 wheeled ATVs, we went up to Cocorná River, which passes beside one of the estates of the Hacienda. There they had five high speed jet skis. Pablo loved doing this, and there was never a visit to the Hacienda in which he didn't dedicate at least two or three hours to bet on races over a long stretch on the Cocorná River. Pablo often raced with my cousin, Gustavo Gaviria, and with every important visitor who came to Napoles. The Atlético Nacional players loved it. They had been invited by my brother after they won the championship of the Copa Libertadores de América.

The best known liberal politicians of the time came to Hacienda Napoles. Beauty queens, famous singers, and acclaimed artists all came to Napoles to entertain our family on weekends and special occasions. Montesinos indulged in every earthly pleasure that Pablo put at his disposal. Although a bit fearful of and inexperienced with regards to watercraft, Montesinos tried a few times to follow behind my brother's jet ski, but always held back on the throttle. We all had an incredible time together, and then we went back to the main house. The day ended with a dip in the swimming pool while listening to the beat of a good samba, and with a cold coconut rum cocktail.

Later, some serious business meetings took place, with Montesinos, my cousin Gustavo, and Pablo. What my brother Pablo wanted was for Montesinos to build a clandestine airstrip in Peru in which his planes could land and take off without any trouble. "The Peruvian Air Force shall not take down my planes," my brother told Ex-Captain Montesinos. He agreed and assured Pablo that this would not be a problem, but the one condition is that he would still need to speak with the high commanders of the Air Force when he returned to Peru. Pablo explained that he would pay for each flight taking off to Colombia with coca paste from his laboratories in the rainforest. "I will let you know from here," Montesinos promised. Pablo shook his hand confidently, like someone who had just sealed a serious business transaction.

The rest of the day they just had personal discussions. My brother told him the story of his life, and the story of Hacienda Napoles, which was like a personal sanctuary. He narrated the way in which the estate used to be entered when the main road had not yet existed, and how the trips had to be done on dirt bikes in order to get to the estate. That originally, Hacienda Napoles had cost him very little money, and then he transformed the estate, bit by bit until it became one of the biggest and most complete in the Magdalena Medio region. He told him that the animals had been bought in a circus that used to come to Colombia, and others had been shipped from Texas, and bought in wildlife farms, legally imported and shipped here. As the import of wild animals was illegal in Colombia, they were brought here in the same planes used for moving the coca paste. The landed in clandestine airstrips from which they were brought to the Hacienda in giant tented trucks with special camouflage cover. Most of the animals were African. In the shipments from the USA, the sellers even advised my brother's workers regarding their care, feeding schedules, and medical reports for each animal. There were species of birds from all around the world in Hacienda Napoles. Pablo wanted to have two of every type of bird in existence. He always wanted to have the quetzal bird, native to Guatemala, and the insignia on the Guatemalan banknote.

Pablo loved animals since he was very little. He and I learned to walk with our dog together. We held his tail, and he started to walk around a tree in our mother's house. We used to call him *Mansor*, because he was placid, and he accompanied us until we were grownups, and then he died. He bought parrots and macaws, and he had one which narrated football matches because Pablo used to sit him beside a big speaker every Sunday at three in the afternoon, when the radio transmission of the Nacional or Medellin matches started. He had bought that bird from some farmers in Puerto Triunfo. As the championships came, that bird learned the names of many of the players mentioned in the transmissions. The only animal that Pablo didn't want to have were cats. In the Hacienda he used to have a mockingbird which used to drink the moonshine leftovers that the rumba guests used to leave, and one time he got drunk after midnight. The mockingbird fell asleep on one of the tables, and when everyone had already gone to bed, an angora cat that was in the house came and ate him. From that moment, Pablo hated cats. He had an omen over a bird which is known as the *cirirí*. A bird of yellow feathers, small and whistled, which mostly ate insects and ticks that the yard animals would always have. When he saw one of these birds, he expressed it was his lucky day.

Montesinos loved the stories narrated by Pablo. At night, he took him to a little bar hidden beside the stable, where Pablo used to have posters of his favorite characters, of his favorite actors and of singers and beauty queens of the time stuck to the wall. Everything in there was vintage. On one side, he took him to see the collection of about 30 old cars: the Fords, Chevrolets, Cadillacs, Mercedes, BMWs, and Plymouths. A bullet-riddled car that was parked in the entrance attracted Montesinos' attention. Pablo explained that it was an old Ford bought in a Medellinean workshop. The way that it was, full of bullet holes, it looked like one of Al Capone's cars. There was even a rumor in the country, which said that Pablo Escobar had bought the famous original car of the mafia boss for millions of dollars.

He told Montesinos that the two cars he liked the most were a 1980 black Mercedes sports car, and a very powerful convertible Porsche. He liked racing cars too, and he took part in the national races at the highest levels. He raced in Cali, Pereira, Medellin and Bogota, with cars he imported from Germany. He was fascinated by speed. He was the first to bring hovercrafts to Colombia that could operate over mud. He was fascinated by the Renault 4 car. He bought them, and he modified them with real rocket engines. With my cousin Gustavo, they participated in several national competitions. Both of them participated in most prestigious races in the so called Copa Renault Championship. He stood out in the races on the Tocancipa racing circuit. He was very close to being crowned national champion until another team mixed water into his racing fuel. This prevented Pablo from winning the points that he needed in the last race of the season.

That night, Montesinos tried the Caldas Rum, and he liked it. Pablo gave him two really big bottles as a gift for him to take to his country. Before midnight, they went to sleep. Montesinos would get up early to travel back to Peru. Pablo said goodbye to him really affectionately, hugged him, and gave him as a gift the white hat he was wearing from the first day of their visit. Montesinos promised he would communicate again within 20 days through a special radio he would send. He said goodbye with his hand up high before closing the door to the plane.

THE OTHER PERUVIAN PLANE

"Chief, a call is coming in, it's Montecristo," *Pinina* told Pablo bringing him the phone. Montesinos' punctuality surprised every single one of us. It had been exactly twenty days since that morning in which the Peruvian Ex-Captain had left from the Napoles hangar, when he promised to make the call which my brother was currently receiving.

"I appreciate your punctuality, Mister Montesinos," Pablo expressed when greeting him. He called to announce to my brother that things were looking good, and that he had already made the appropriate contacts. The next step was to install a radiophone close to the airstrip, in order to finalize the arrangements.

Twenty days later, Montesinos called again. He notified Pablo that everything had been organized according to Pablo's request, and that Pablo should send him a radio. Pablo got excited and recognized that Montesinos was the perfect man to do business with. Earnest, trustworthy and efficient. "Tell me how, when and where to send the radio," my brother told the Peruvian. They arranged a specific place in Panama City, where the device would be bought. There, an emissary of Pablo made the purchase and the shipping arrangements to the Peruvian territory that Montesinos had planned for the clandestine airstrip, deep in the Peruvian rainforest. Business was now ready to begin. The airstrip, the link, and the radiophone were ready. Only the coca paste and the planes were missing. My brother took care of that.

In less than a month, the first flights arrived. Everything was coordinated through the radiophone given to Montesinos. The calls, almost always, were made between Montesinos and Pablo. Montesinos distributed, amongst his workers, the money that Pablo sent to pay for the salaries. Pablo and Montesinos had agreed that for every *crowned* kilo, which is, that departed from Peru and arrived to Colombia without any trouble, $300 dollars would be for the workers at the Peruvian airstrip. With each trip, they would be dealing in amounts in the range of $100,000 to $120,000 dollars. The sum could vary depending on the plane size. Of that gross amount, 40 percent went to Montesinos. The remaining 60 percent, was distributed by Montesinos among the military men in Peru who allowed business to be conducted. All the money was given to Montesinos in a hotel or in apartments in Panama City, where my brother used to have very good contacts. Other times, the captain required the money to be delivered to a location in Miami, and an envoy of my brother who rented a place in Miami would handle the transaction. The only condition he presented was for the money to be delivered in cash in US dollars. They had arranged to never perform any bank transactions. In general, large sums of cash were delivered at the Marriot Hotel in Panama City. It was a lot of money, because my brother sent between three and four planes daily, which returned the same day.

Things were working perfectly. Montesinos was our most important man in Peru, and a great friend of the Peruvian political and military leadership. Pablo had Montesinos monitored, and friends of his in Peru kept Pablo informed about what the Ex-Captain did in the Peruvian capital. "He had become a good friend, but in matters related to money, any good man can change," Pablo explained when he referred to Montesinos. "We have to keep an eye on him." The Ex-Captain's movements were in some way followed by associates of Pablo, to avoid any unexpected surprises. What my brother was sure about, was that Montesinos definitely had direct access to the authorities in Peru. He actually was, as he had told us, a "well-trusted man among military men." Everyone followed the reports he gave to my brother, they paid attention to his intel, and he became a sort of advisor with regards to Peruvian government secrets and inside information on Peruvian leadership.

The relationship with our friend Montesinos couldn't be any better. Everyone came out ahead. Montesinos because of the good money he was receiving, and Pablo because of the ease with which he was bringing coca paste into Colombia. Montesinos made sure that the Peruvian Air Force stayed away from our operation. Pablo's planes were actually well received in Peru. However, we found out that other traffickers, which belonged to different organizations, were attacked and chased out of Peru. According to Montesinos, they had to show good results to the press, and that's why once in a while a plane with coca paste had to be intercepted. The idea was not to raise suspicion among Americans.

One afternoon while Pablo was in Napoles, we received an unexpected call from Montesinos. Pablo was listening to him, and because of the look on Pablo's face, we knew that it was really good news. He told us within minutes after ending the call, that the Ex-Captain had revealed that he had now become a close friend of a man, who was an emerging Presidential candidate. It was an engineer of Japanese origin, who was really well liked among the Peruvian people. According to Montesinos, he would undoubtedly become the next President. Pablo always recognized in Montesinos that he was a visionary with a futurist mindset. "That guy thinks about everything, and is always one step ahead of us," my brother said. He was referring to the fact that Montesinos was already securing a spot as the right-hand man of a possible President, and how it would not only guarantee the continuity of the coca paste business, but also set the stage to broaden our horizons.

So things kept moving along smoothly. Montesinos was beginning to become more absent from overseeing operations at the Peruvian airstrips, but Pablo understood that he was devoted to politics. Pablo liked that, and the political campaigns were almost in full swing. Later when the expected call would arrive, Montesinos told my brother that things were going well politically, just as expected and in a matter of days he would ask for a personal favor, which would be very important for everyone involved. Pablo understood, and he waited for Montesinos to call him back. Montesinos called my brother, and he explained that his friend, Alberto Fujimori, would need money for his political campaign. "Please assist me in funding his campaign," Montesinos told him. Without hesitation Pablo agreed, and asked for instructions on how to send the money. He explained that it should be sent in the same planes that were being used to transport the coca paste, and the money should arrive at the same airstrips. The idea was not to do it through Panama or Miami, in order to not raise any suspicion with the authorities, Montesinos explained. "How much does Fujimoro need?" Pablo asked. "One million dollars," Montesinos replied. "Cash, if possible," the Ex-Captain highlighted to my brother.

Pablo immediately agreed, and he called Medellin to prepare the money for transport. He ordered two of his men to pack the money. A million dollars cash doesn't go unnoticed. I remembered that he sent the money in several carton boxes, to disguise the cash as newly packed televisions. Montesinos picked up the money personally. I'm sure that the money arrived at Fujimori's campaign headquarters because days later Engineer Fujimori himself called Pablo to thank him for the gesture. I answered that call myself, an afternoon in which my brother and I were watching herd in the Puerto Triunfo area, very close to Hacienda Napoles. We travelled in a white Daihatsu all-terrain vehicle which had a mobile phone installed that was legally authorized by the Department of Enterprises in Antioquia. The number, which I can still remember, was 720222. I answered the call from Montesinos, I greeted him with respect and passed the phone to my brother. It was about six in the afternoon, and my brother was wearing a Medellinean hat, and he had a poncho draped over his shoulder. It was very hot and humid. The mosquitos were already biting. "My Captain Montesinos," Pablo greeted him over the phone. They talked about how well business was going in both countries. Pablo asked about his friend and about the gift that he had received, and Montesinos thanked Pablo for the gesture. Later, Pablo changed the friendly tone of his voice, to talk in a more diplomatic tone. "My dear President, good afternoon," he told Engineer Fujimori who was already talking. They conversed for 10 minutes time, and my brother also raised the subject of politics. "I like politics, Mr. Fujimori, and I work for the people too," he told him. He explained that he was politically liberal and left-leaning, and that he hoped someday they would meet to discuss the topic more deeply. Pablo told him he that he read a lot about European liberalism, and that his idea was to fight from the highest levels of Government to end social inequality. He told him that, during his trips to Europe, he once had the chance to attend the assumption of a Spanish president as a special guest of the P.S.O.E. political party, and that he thought many advanced ideas of European liberalism could be applied to the poor countries of Latin America such as Peru and Colombia. "That there is misery in our countries is one thing, but we should fight for it not to be there anymore," Pablo told Fujimori in an almost campaign-speech tone, as if he was talking to a large crowd in the middle of a Sunday park instead of the future Peruvian president. "I want to be the President of Colombia too, and someday we will both be Presidents together," he told Fujimori. Later, in a more reverential tone, he put his planes, his money and his contacts in Colombia at Fujimori's disposal. He said goodbye very respectfully, and he insisted again for Fujimori to count on his help for anything, and that arrangements would be done through Montesinos. They said goodbye, and Pablo kept talking to Montesinos.

It wasn't the only time Pablo talked personally with Engineer Fujimori. It happened again two or three more times. Pablo was deeply grateful to Montesinos for the important contact that he had made, and from then on, Pablo felt more confident about him. The shipments kept moving without any problems. Planes would come and go.

The Peruvian coca paste, the most appreciated in the world, was landing every day in the laboratories. Trucks with patrols of men and women picked up the paste at the airstrips, and took them in loads to the rainforest where Pablo had built the *kitchens*, where the paste was processed and converted into pure cocaine, fresh and ready to be exported. The *kitchens* were almost like fortresses, with rooms for 100 people or more, which had all of the amenities that one could ever need. They had bedrooms, cabins, dining rooms, entertaining and playing areas and the heating rooms, which were the most isolated places where the drug was subjected to the different steps of the process. Each one of these locations had 200 or more microwaves, suitable not for heating food but instead used to give the drug a bit more firmness. The workers were brought from Medellin or the outer territories, and they earned a really good salary, had free food, and free boarding. The workers had 15 days per year for holidays, and despite the work days being long and hard, they were well compensated in wages. The arrival of the drug paste depended on the plane shipments from Peru. Montesinos knew all about the cocaine conversion process, and decided to speed up the amount of shipments. But he delegated this task to his men, which were his military friends. He wasn't present at the Peruvian airstrips anymore, because he was always with Fujimori.

One afternoon, at an airstrip owned by my brother in Envigado, the telephone rang. A guy named Carlos answered, and he passed the device to Pablo. "Chief, it's Montecristo," he told him. My brother took the phone and on the other side, Montesinos greeted him, "Good afternoon, Doctor." Pablo and he had agreed that he would always refer to my brother as *Mister* or *Doctor*, to answer without any trouble.

That day, my brother noticed Montesinos was a little drunk, because his words were slurred and his explanations were inconsistent. However, Pablo understood. He was celebrating the victory of Alberto Fujimori, who had just been elected the new Peruvian president. "We won, he's President," he told my brother in the middle of the commotion of a party which had just started.

The relationship among them became stronger than ever. Before surrendering to the authorities, my brother talked with Montesinos about the future of the business, and the Ex-Captain advised him to travel to Peru instead of surrendering, that there he and his friend President Fujimori would give him safety and tranquility for my brother and the family.

"This is a message for President Fujimori¸" Pablo clarified his intentions to Montesinos. "No thank you, Captain, please tell the president that I will not be leaving Colombia," my brother answered. He explained that the safest place for him to be is likely in Antioquia, Medellin. "I also have people who want to protect me here," he told Montesinos. Pablo then thanked him for the gesture, and he asked him to thank President Fujimori from Pablo Escobar and the entire Escobar family. He insisted on letting the new Peruvian State boss know that he could count on indefinite support, even if he was in jail. "It's better for me not to be in Peru, because if they capture me in your homeland, it will be damaging for both you and the President," he expressed. Besides, the risk of being captured in Peru made it more possible for extradition to the USA, something that would be more difficult in Colombia.

There are a lot of witnesses who can corroborate what I have said. Several of the men, who worked for Fujimori and his people even supported my brother's coca flights. The DEA must have had information on at least two shipments, which departed from Montesinos' airstrips and eventually ended up in the USA. One of these shipments, for example, arrived at an Amazonian airstrip, and from there was loaded on to a wooden ship in La Florida, Colombia. This cargo was later unloaded in Tampa, Florida in a DEA operation. As a result of this shipment, several of Pablo's workers went to prison for a long time. If I remember correctly, on that ship they had about 3,000 kilos of cocaine. There was also another ship, which had cocaine hidden in fish flour. The flour was bought in Ecuador, and the drug was put in before taking it to the airstrips. Montesinos knew all of the routes, and when the shipment went out directly to La Florida, or when it made a layover in Colombia. Both he and Fujimori knew about, which eventually led to their downfall.

CEDRAS'S FRIEND

Pablo's relationships were always of the highest caliber. He had direct contact with several national leaders and Presidents in both Central and South America; with dictators, with prime ministers, with generals, and other important politicians. Raúl Cedrás, for example the dictator of Haiti, who came to power after President Aristide's exile, was also on my brother's payroll. Before he became dictator, Cedrás was Commander-In-Chief of the Haitian Armed Forces. Pablo knew how important the island was because of its strategic location for moving drugs to the USA.

Despite not meeting him in person, he kept a good telephone based relationship with Cedrás. He had come to know him through a worker of his, who travelled to the island frequently. Cedrás controlled everything. While he controlled the Armed Forces,

Cedrás collaborated with my brother Pablo in delivering confidential and secret information, such as when certain areas of Haiti and its waters would be free of US forces or free from US observation. He designated an airstrip for my brother so that his planes would arrive in the morning, and left without being detected. The drug arrived at the island and then it was re-packed in boxes disguised as the native rum of Puerto Principe, which was famous worldwide. For each plane which landed there without any trouble and managed to leave, my brother paid $10,000 in cash. The estate with the airstrip belonged to some of Cedras' friends, and many politicians supported Pablo too.

NORIEGA, THE BETRAYER

Perhaps the key Government official with whom Pablo received more support in the drug business than anybody else was Gereral Noriega in Panama. He had meet him in person in 1981 in the Panamanian capital. He was introduced to him through another high official in the Armed Forces, whose last name was Melo. Noriega enabled my brother's helicopters to land in the capital's airports. The helicopters departed from Medellin, picked up the merchandise and, after loading fuel in the Choco rainforest, they continued to Panama City, where they were received without any problem. They practically landed in the Panamanian streets themselves. A large part of the money produced by the business arrived in Panama. Many times on commercial flights, on ships, in submarines, or in the drug planes themselves. Sometimes transactions were made from well-known banks in the USA with subsidiaries in Panama City. The money was collected and brought to Colombia in helicopters. The money arrived in Colombia, and was collected in small airports in Antioquia, Caldas or Tolima. Many times, the airport closest to the Napoles estate was chosen, in order for it to be transported by car after it landed. One of my brother's preferred airports was the Mariquita airport. The area was world famous because of its fruits, and the town had a charming tranquility to it. The planes or helicopters full of dollars arrived in Mariquita, and the money was transported from there in cars headed to Dorada, Medellin, or Bogota.

Panama was very important because of its closeness to the Choco rainforest in Colombia. The cargos were rarely intercepted. As far as I can remember, there was only one time in which my brother blamed Noriega directly because his men were careless. There was a big load, for which the general had received a payoff of $1,500,000. Noriega himself had to figure out how to get rid of this problem at the judicial level because several men had been captured by the Panamanian authorities. Among the prisoners that I remember very well there was *Jhon Lada*, a really trustworthy young man. In order to set him free, Noriega had to make the judge believe it was a legal load of Colombian sugar instead of drugs. For that purpose, he asked my brother to send him boxes full of salt and sugar in the same way he had sent the drugs, and they hired witnesses to attest during the hearing that it was merely only sugar coming into Panama. The judge believed them, and all of men in jail were released. It is worth mentioning that today, every single one of them is dead. Noriega received a lot of money from my brother Pablo. He billed for everything. For each helicopter which arrived or left, for every plane depending on the size, for the people who entered the country and left, and for the money which came in and out. Noriega took a cut on everything that he could. Now despite my brother knowing that Noriega was not the most trustworthy man, he would still prove to be useful in one particular emergency situation.

In this case, after the death of Colombian Justice Minister Rodrigo Lara, drug dealers were immediately blamed for his murder. As a result, many of the Colombian capos immediately travelled to Panamanian territory. Pablo, *El Mexicano*, my cousin Gustavo, Carlos Lehder, the Ochoas, and even the Cali cartel were there. At that time, the wars between the cartels had not yet begun. Panama was, for Pablo and his friends, an endless paradise. There were banks for moving money, luxury hotels, cars, personal security, ease of doing business and, above all, powerful friends. Pablo was staying at the main house of General Noriega. He had a beautiful mansion with security detail, full of antiques and military objects which belonged to his friend, Noriega. His medallions, distinctions, sabers and photos of his most memorable moments were hanging from the brilliant walls of the home. There was a swimming pool, tennis courts, football courts, and a running track. The mansion adjoined the Country Club, the most exclusive area of the city, surrounded by tranquility and civility. In the morning, in front of the country club, it was pretty normal to see all of the mafia bosses of the time jogging. *El Mexicano* wore colorful lycra underpants, brand new tennis shoes, and he had a headband so that his hair would avoid flying in his face. My brother was on a bike and doing pushups. My cousin Gustavo played tennis. Carlos Lehder read his morning newspaper while smoking weed. Chauffeurs drove all of the capos in beautiful cars, while pedestrians had the look of astonishment on their faces as they couldn't distinguish if we were a group of Colombian travelers or a group of drug dealers evading extradition back to Colombia, or even worse extradition to the USA. This level of comfort didn't come for free. My brother gave Noriega

$5,000,000 dollars. The money included the building costs for a new clandestine airstrip that Pablo wanted Noriega to keep ready in the Darien, which was more strategically located for planes to come in and out of Panama. He sent the money with three Colombians, who scheduled an appointment with Colonel Melo in the lobby of the Holiday Inn Hotel, or near Punta Paitilla. The Colonel gave the money to Noriega in a private home, and then Noriega would distribute the money among his most trusted officials, who also collaborated in Pablo's business. Logically, the General took the lion's share, because he was the Commander-In-Chief.

A few days after the arrival to the Panamanian capital, Pablo sent for myself, my son José Roberto, the wife of my cousin Gustavo, and Pablo's wife, María Victoria, who was about to give birth. It was María Victoria's first pregnancy. He sent a helicopter from Panama; the same helicopter in which he had travelled.

We departed in the morning, but we had to land in the middle of the rainforest, in Darien, very close to the place everyone says Jaime Bateman Cayón was killed. The weather was bad, but the reason for the layover was a leak coming from either the fuel tank or the fuel line. We lost almost all of our fuel, and we had to land. It was very foggy. We stayed sitting next to the helicopter, and we had some canned food for lunch, which María Victoria had brought as a precaution. We waited until three o'clock, and as time went by, the concern and the anxiety increased, especially for the pregnant María Victoria, and for my son José Roberto. We imagined Pablo's own despair as he waited for us in Panama, but we trusted something would happen soon. Around 4:30 that afternoon, we saw a helicopter, and we composed ourselves. We quickly helped the women and children to climb aboard. The copilot, a worker, and I stayed there. Because it was almost night time, we knew the helicopter wasn't going to come back for us that day. We organized our camp for the night so that we could sleep in the middle of the rainforest, accompanied only by the sound of the strange animals and the shadows cast by the moonlight as it had started to outline the tips of the tall trees of that immaculate jungle. The following day, the same helicopter came for us, and we departed to Panama City around eleven in the morning.

We all arrived at different houses in the city. We travelled on motorbikes, and in cars with dark, tinted windows. In the beginning, Pablo didn't want Noriega to know about our presence there. He did not fully trust the general. Pablo never owned any properties in Panama. He made all of the real estate purchases through third party straw buyers. He didn't want to have any verifiable legal links to General Noriega, and he knew it was a risk that he couldn't afford to take. "Noriega himself may take it all away at any moment," he used to say.

We stayed there for three months, until Pablo received information that Noriega was willing to betray him. A colonel of the Panamanian Army alerted him. Noriega commented during secret meetings that it was possible to negotiate with the Americans in exchange for immunity. If Noriega needed a wildcard, he was willing to give up Pablo to the DEA as a last resort move to protect himself. My brother was very worried, especially for the safety of our families, and he ordered everyone to return to Colombia as soon as possible. He sent everybody to Paitilla airport in the morning, where he had parked his private plane, a Comander 1000. At five o'clock in the morning, the entire family fled from Panama. Pablo left a few hours later, after trying to communicate with Noriega that he was quite upset to learn that he would be willing to hand him over to the DEA. Pablo made a bold statement to one of the Panamanian Colonels. "Tell Noriega that I want my money back!" Then he returned to Medellin.

In Colombia, he called him again, and this time he communicated, "General, you were gonna betray me?" He demanded the immediate refund of the money. "I will give you three days to send the money to Medellin." Right away, Pablo sent a warning which Noriega must have felt like a kick to the stomach, "If you fail to give me my money back within the time that I've just given to you, I will go to Panama myself, I will take you on a plane, and I will send you to the USA immediately." Pablo meant it, and Noriega knew that the threat was real. He accepted. Three days later, two workers of my brother received an envoy of Noriega who left a private plane at Olaya Herrera airport with two heavy suitcases. He was the son of a Panamanian General. They received him, and they accommodated him in the Intercontinental Hotel. Pablo's instructions were to count the money, banknote by banknote. The Noriega chapter had ended. Later on, the same colonel, who informed Pablo about the betrayal, would tell Pablo that Noriega had been the one who gave the Colombian authorities all of the information that led to the capture of the famous *Karina* ship, in which the M-19 had attempted to bring a huge and powerful arsenal into the country.

PABLO AND COLOMBIAN POLITICIANS

Pablo Escobar was an innate politician. From the time when he was little, I noticed that he loved speaking to crowds. At school, he used to distribute food among the kids who didn't have anything to eat.

In High School, he led student protests. With his speeches, he overthrew teachers who were entrenched in arcane teaching methods. He was the president of the Communal Action Board in the neighborhood where we were raised, and his political aspiration was to reach the Envigado Council. Some well-known political leaders of Antioquia saw the compassion in him, and the ease in which he was able to reach the most disenfranchised areas of the city. This was precisely how he unintentionally entered into politics. One Saturday morning at the gasoline station, Pablo asked a young guy, who was washing his Renault 4, where he lived. "I don't live, I survive in my landfill," the young man answered. Pablo didn't believe him in the beginning, but the guy explained to him with further details that he lived together with a group of very poor families beside the city landfill, and that they subsisted on finding used items that they found among the waste of rich Medellinean people. He explained that he alternated his time with washing cars studying so that he could finish high school. Pablo was moved, and he ask him to bring him to where he lived. The young man accepted, and they arranged a visit for the following Saturday. Pablo went there accompanied by an uncle, who was very popular reporter in Medellin, and he saw the young man's living situation first hand. My brother was shocked at what he saw because even though my mother had raised us in the midst of poverty, we had never known misery. From that day onward, Pablo used to say that, "A country can have all of the poverty in the world, but misery should never be tolerated." Pablo's visit to the landfill inspired him to fight for those people, and take them away from that wretched state of life. Every week on Saturday or Sunday, he visited those people, and he brought them gifts. He purchased food and gifts for the children, and he gave them to the people as he talked about the challenges of fighting to end the social inequality that Colombia had. Soon, his ability to lead really started to shine. He became a leader in the community, and people searched for Pablo to get advice on how to improve their lives. They invited Pablo to have lunch at a street fair they had organized. People gathered in the streets, and each family participated by cooking something to eat. They cooked massive meals on the firewood, and drank beer. It was a meal that fed everyone in the neighborhood, and an act of integration into the community. That day, honoring Pablo, they prepared chicken soup which they served in old broken dishes. Pablo enjoyed the meal and asked one of the old ladies how they came to prepare the food. "We find everything in the trash, Doctor," the woman answered. Pablo was not even slightly perturbed, and he thanked again for the gesture of having him as an honored guest. "It's not fair that, while you have to feed yourselves with trash from the city, rich people are eating in the best restaurants at the Medellin Country Club," he told them. This experience was useful for solidifying the bond that had already been formed between the community and Pablo. From that moment on, it was imperative for my brother to bring them the food every week. "I'm gonna build a neighborhood for you, a real neighborhood!" The landfill neighborhood leaders, who heard him cheerfully shouted his name. The work started immediately. He rented an office in the area where the architects advised him on which areas had stable ground to build on. In a matter of weeks, things were moving along. He planned the construction of about 500 houses in several stages. "The first houses will be for the elders, the orphans and the abandoned women," he explained to them in the evening meetings that he attended and which were also accompanied by his uncle, Hernando Gaviria, and by a cousin who was already engaged in politics, named José Obdulio.

"Pablo, why don't you engage in politics? The people love you so much," our cousin insisted. Pablo had already thought of that, and he knew about the people's affection for him, and he agreed. "Yes, I'm going to run for office because the money in this country has been stolen by politicians." While he moved forward with construction in the neighborhood, Pablo was also making himself known to the Antioquian political class and several of the best-known politicians of the country. He became friends with Jairo Ortega, a prestigious liberal leader with a congressional seat, and who would become a springboard for my brother at the national level. Up to that moment, Pablo was seduced by local and regional politics, but with Ortega he broaden his horizons and significantly raised his aspirations. Now, Pablo thought he was unstoppable. The elections came, and they formed a new political party. Pablo agreed to be the second member of the new party, after Doctor Ortega. His original goal from the beginning, was simply to be an Envigado counselor, but his friends convinced him to go for something bigger. "You have to start from below," he used to say. But expert political analysts knew that Pablo's popular acclaim was enough to have him elected to the Congress of the Republic. Ortega went first and Pablo went second on their list of the newly created *Renovación Liberal* political party (*Liberal Renewal*). In only two months, they had received a historic amount of 17,000 votes.

When he finally had the opportunity to enter Congress, already authorized as a Congressman, he had his first argument, even before entering the building. The doorman didn't want to let him in because he wasn't wearing a tie. "It's a rule for everyone, Sir," the doorman said. Pablo thought that perhaps the little doorman took notice to Pablo's Medellinean accent, denim trousers, plain-looking shoes, and short-sleeved shirt and did not believe that he was actually a Congressman of the Republic. Pablo explained that wearing a tie doesn't mean anything. The stubbornness of the doorman carried more weight than my brother's arguments. Finally Pablo gave up. In his jacket pocket he carried an old tie. He asked a lawyer who was beside him to tie the knots, and he adjusted it. He entered the building, after thirty minutes of discussion. Inside, once he was in his Congressional seat, he took his tie off. Everyone was looking at him like a freak, but he persisted with his head high. Today, many Congressmen enter and leave without a tie, and even others, such as indigenous people, imposed their way of dressing and their traditional clothes.

In Congress, he met other distinguished politicians. Pablo believed in their abilities as politicians, but as time went on, he discovered that most of these politicians were hypocrites looking to line their own pockets with money. One of them was Alberto Santofimio Botero, an astute Tolimanian political leader, with a loud voice and powerful political ties. Pablo recognized in him that he was a man with sufficient ability to climb to the highest levels of politics, convincing and above all, nimble in his speech management. With great ease he was able to speak in public squares and manipulate all of his followers into listening to him. But Santofimio, the same as many other politicians of the time, was an ambitious man, who liked money, power, and pleasure above politics and people. In the midst of the pre-presidential candidacy fervor, Pablo saw the dark side of this man. Santofimio asked him for economic support for his presidential candidacy, and Pablo agreed. Pablo raised some money with other drug dealer friends in Medellin, and he sent this money to Santofimio. After receiving the money, Santofimio announced his retirement from the campaign and he told Pablo that he should support the official candidate of the liberal party. Santofimio explained to my brother that the problem was the division of the party, and his role was to support the party. Pablo didn't accept his arguments. He didn't use the money he had already given him for his personal campaign either. Santofimio was effectively a hypocrite, while other politicians did have good intentions. At the time, Pablo had hobnobbed with national figures of great stature, and during the presidential campaign, he helped two other candidates. In Envigado, he even had lunch with Belisario Betancur. Pablo discussed his ideas, and with enthusiasm he told Belisario about the neighborhood that he was about to build. Some time later, the then attorney Carlos Jiménez Gómez and other distinguished politicians, would attend a meeting in a well-known luxury hotel of Panama, City, where they would listen to my brother and other drug dealers' proposal to pay for the sum total of the external debt of the country, in exchange for a non-extradition law to be passed in Colombia. I must admit that it was an intervention of humanitarian nature, backed by good intentions and my brother's love for Colombia. During the meeting, my brother kept bringing up his community development activities for the neighborhood, for which Pablo had just chosen the name, *Medellin Sin Tugurios* (*Medellin Without Slums*). At the time, the conservative candidate for presidency wanted to harvest crops with foreign compost, and started to introduce himself to the people of the landfill neighborhood that my brother had been working on developing. The idea was to have an opening ceremony with great fanfare, but circumstances prevented this from happening. Pablo knew about the Conservative party's intentions, and he underscored the urgent need to finish construction of the first houses. He identified the people most in need of housing, and he delivered the houses to them in a non-stop, marathon-like effort that he was forced to perform in just a matter of days. He knew about the intentions of some of the conservative leaders to encroach upon the almost finished neighborhood. The conservative leaders used to say that the construction of the neighborhood should be stopped because it had been built with "hot" money. "When the money is for them, it's considered cold, but when it's for poor people in a landfill, it's considered hot," he answered them. So, he delivered the first houses, which came with a television, a refrigerator, a heater, and all of the basic home services. The big grand opening that he had planned to give to his neighborhood could not be done. Eventually the neighborhood was completed, and Pablo was able to eradicate part of the country's misery in the poorest of neighborhoods. Pablo did a lot for Colombia's poor.

His time spent as a congressman brought him much heartache. While he did meet some good and helpful people, he also met some bad people, like Doctor Belisario, who turned out to be another one of the hypocrite politicians of the day, despite being the conservative candidate. I remember well that, through one of his advisors, he asked my brother to lend him a plane for touring around Antioquia. Pablo and *El Mexicano* agreed with pleasure, and they put a modern plane at his disposal, which they sent from Medellin. According to his advisors, Doctor Belisario wanted the plane to have the traditional paint of the conservatives, and he asked for it to be painted blue and white, just like the conservative flag. Pablo didn't see a problem, but *El Mexicano* did get angry. "*These politicians are sometimes totally shameless,*" Gonzalo Rodríguez told my brother. But the plane was painted, and it was sent on the campaign trail. Ironically, that same plane would be captured by the authorities with *El Mexicano* on board in an airport close to Bogota.

Double standards are very common among politicians. That was also the case with our cousin José Obdulio. When I was prisoner in

Itagui jail, I used to share the same yard with the guerrilla leaders, Francisco *Pacho* Galán, Francisco *Pacho* Carballo, and Felipe Torres. They were interesting guys with whom I held a good relationship. We used to talk about the country, and the potential ways to achieve peace, an issue they had been working on with the Government. They used to receive in the jail, all the people who wanted to collaborate with them to achieve peace in Colombia. They worked with the Human Rights groups, the Congress and the Church commissions. That's how Isaías Duarte Cancino and my cousin José Obdulio Gaviría showed up there one morning, accompanied by other peace negotiators. From my cell, I sent some tasty snacks and beverages to make their meeting better. I did not have access to the area of the jail where Galán and the others had gathered, Through a fence next to the yard where I was, one of the people present in the meeting told me that my cousin, José Obdulio, had just denied that we were relatives. According to my informer, someone had told José Obdulio that in the same yard was his cousin, Roberto, and that he should pass by his cell to greet him later. According to the person who was telling me the story, José Obdulio told the people in the meeting that he didn't have any relatives named Roberto Escobar, and that it was really weird to be told that. After hearing this, I waited for their meeting to end, and when they were leaving the jail, through the side of my jail cell, I leaned my head to scream to my cousin, "Did you hear, José Obdulio, that when you were coming up to La Catedral, my brother gave you money? Back then you were my cousin, but now, not anymore," and everyone looked at José with mockery and with surprise. He used to go to visit us in La Catedral and Pablo used to give him 10 million or 15 million pesos for his personal and political affairs in Medellin. José Obdulio's father is my mother's brother, and we've always received him as just another relative. But my brother never received our cousin with a hidden agenda. Pablo gave him money with the intention of helping him to grow. This was all part of my brother's experience as a politician in Colombia. It was brief, but very productive. On a personal level, he achieved part of what he had always dreamed of, to lift many people out of misery. In his political career, he was exposed to the poorest people in Colombia while at the same time rubbing elbows with world figures, such as the Spanish president, Felipe González himself. Today, I'm confident that, if he had the chance to continue on his path, my brother would have been president of this country. Today I remember with certain nostalgia, phrases of the song which my aunt, Blanca Gaviria, my mother's sister, wrote for my brother when he jumped into the political arena. "When they pass by his side, he stretches his hands to everyone, he gives to the poor and to the helpless and that's why they remember him with affection intoning this song. Pablo, I'm begging you, please don't engage in politics anymore, that those politicians are going to betray you."

The verses of that song were prescient, because not only was Pablo betrayed by the Government, by his military and police friends, but also by the politicians who stuck to his side. My mother still remembers the Santofimio and Jairo Ortega cases, and even William Vélez, who she assures obtained his seat in Congress thanks to Pablo. According to her, this William Vélez was about to steal a car from my brother, who had lent it to him for the campaign. Pablo searched for several months for that politician so that he would give the car back.

My father, who usually stayed away from any of our business, would berate me for having trusted everyone, and Pablo too for having believed in the words of politicians, and for having surrendered to Justice, because he knew that the Gaviria Government had betrayed him when he surrendered to La Catedral. Our father never agreed with that initial surrender, "Colombia is too big for hiding," he warned us.

THE LAST TRIP

With Pablo, we used to talk daily through the mobile phone that he had brought to my prison. He had moved to a new house, and he stayed there alone, isolated from the family, and accompanied only by cousin Lucila, the daughter of a sister of my mother. With the family, he used to maintain communication through mail, which at that time became less frequent. He hated being alone, and he suffered greatly because he could not really have too much personal contact with our mother and the others. The telephone contact was each time more risky. We had received information from an official of the Search Block, according to which the equipment that the DEA had could be used to locate Pablo at any moment. "The only way to find your brother is through the mobile phone calls that he makes," the official told us. Pablo asked me for a mobile phone to be able to communicate more often with our mother and the kids. He told me to send a worker of mine, the most trustworthy, so that he accompanied him during his evening outings. "I don't like to walk alone," he told me. By then, *El Angelito* and *El Chopo* had already died, two of the guys that had accompanied him in the past few days, in the hardest part of his persecution.

I thought about Álvaro, one of my butlers, whom we affectionately called *Limón* (*Lemon*). Álvaro had recently written me asking me to let him work with my brother again. We didn't want to bring him to La Catedral, because we needed him to be clean of any ties to my brother. That day, I decided Álvaro was the key man for Pablo. I set an appointment with him in the jail, and I explained to him what his new task was. "That's what I've always wanted, to work with the boss again," he told me as he was visibly happy with the news that I had just given to him. I told him how to reach the house where Pablo was staying. Before he met him, I asked him to go to a place in the center of Medellin to pick up a portable phone, which Pablo needed urgently. Before saying goodbye, I gave him a letter written in my own handwriting, addressed to my brother. "Don't talk on the phone, don't talk on the phone, don't talk on the phone," the letter prayed along its whole length. Like this, I wanted to let him know that, despite the fact that I was sending him the phone, it was too risky to use because of the warning they had given me. It was November 17th. Limón went out, and I reaffirmed the safety precautions he was supposed to take. The situation wasn't the best one. The new house in which my brother hid was located close to the stadium, in an area known as *Los Olivos* (*The olive trees*).

Pablo had bought a taxi, waiting for *Limón*'s arrival. He became his driver, escort and friend. At night, well-disguised, with his thick beard, glasses, and moustache, Pablo went out in the taxi but not to the avenues of the center of the city anymore. Rather, Pablo went to the popular and isolated neighborhoods of the city. He preferred the San Javier neighborhood, and he frequented a store with chairs in the street, in which he used to drink dark coffee and eat bread.

Cousin Lucila used to prepare him the food. "Of all of them, that one's the tastiest," Pablo used to repeat when he recalled the family parties in which the cousin was in charge of making the dessert buffet, and the pound cake. She was the foremost expert in baking cookies for birthdays. She made them in all sizes and colors, except for chocolate. My brother hated chocolate.

Limón may have added to the tension that Pablo was becoming absorbed in. He believed in witches, in fairies, in four-leaf clovers, in curses, in bindings, in witchcraft, and whatever else had to do with the esoteric world. This cousin would tell me, months later, that Pablo had much fun with *Limón*'s notes about his supposed predictions about the good and the bad. On the afternoon of November 30th, around four o'clock, Pablo was sitting in a chair reading the newspaper and a black hairy fly visited him. He sat on his right arm and then hovered over him like he was analyzing Pablo. My brother was overweight. He was eating more than he should, especially rice and fried bananas. Maybe the stress made him gain all of that weight. His stomach was more prominent, and the double chin could not seem to hide below his beard. Pablo folded the newspaper and started trying to swat the fly. Pablo tried his best to kill the fly, but the fly was moving too quickly. The insect turned out to be more agile and astute, and that's when *Limón* intervened. The fly was relentless and sought after my brother. He came back, and he placed his little body on Pablo's leg. *Limón* put on a concerned face. "Generally, when that happens, bad news is coming," he revealed. My brother answered with a big laugh, and he asked him to get rid of the bug. *Limón* enclosed him in a corner of the room, he opened the window and guided him out of the house, and then he closed the window. The fly was gone.

At night, Pablo asked cousin Lucila to buy a book as a gift for me. It was the last version of the Guinness Book of Records. Lucila bought the book in a nearby shopping mall, and she gave it to Pablo in the hall. In the central table, Pablo took a pen and wrote something on the first page, after the main cover. He gave it back to the cousin, he told her to pack it in gift wrap and send it to me. He explained that was a good way to become aware of the latest events in the sports world. Pablo and I used to send each other messages with sports stories, with names of famous players, with dates of historic events, and with results of unforgettable matches. He forced me to keep well informed, in order not to lose his sports bets. He knew the line ups of the best teams in the world, the players that scored the big goals, the winners, and the final scores of the championship games.

At 11:30 at night, they went out again, this time on foot. They came back at four in the morning. Pablo prayed aloud and then went to sleep. The following day, December 1st, he woke up at one in the afternoon. It was his birthday. He had his favorite dish for breakfast, rice mixed with eggs, and fried bananas. He drank coffee and he ate an *arepa*. He read all the letters he had been sent from the night before, and he memorized the cards from his wife and kids, who wrote beautiful words about the strength of life, and how this New Year's Eve would be spent beside him. "Despite you're not here, for us you're still hidden in a corner in our hearts. Happy birthday. I love you daddy," Manuela wrote him. Juan Pablo reminded him how important he was in his life, and he assured Pablo that he would keep praying at night until he could have him by his side. María Victoria thanked him for the years that he dedicated to her in the beginning of their life together, she stamped a kiss over the paper, and she asked him to love her for the rest of his years. He would turn 42.

At three, he asked Lucila to go to the Éxito and buy the ingredients for a lasagna with chicken, some French bread, and a Veuve

Clicquot Champagne bottle. The cousin came back an hour later, and she prepared lasagna with her best seasoning. They ate in the dining room beside the hall, and Pablo asked *Limón* to uncork the bottle, but he couldn't do it. My brother took the bottle with a dry cloth, and hit it against the wall. The cork shot out and fell just over *Limón*'s head. "Thank goodness it wasn't a weapon, boss," he said smiling. She remind him, that they were only three in the house. Pablo toasted. "There are only three of us, but the wineglass symbolizes the presence of the family who's not accompanying me today." The three of them raised their arms, and the wineglasses sounded. "For my family, for everyone's welfare," Pablo added before drinking. "Happy birthday, Chief," *Limón* said. "May God protect you forever," cousin Lucila told him. They hugged him. The cousin brought a birthday cake from the kitchen, which she had prepared for him. "Don't worry, Pablo, it's a vanilla cake, and it doesn't have chocolate." So *Limón* asked for a new toast. This time, for having the opportunity to work with my brother again. "God put us on each other's path," he said. Pablo thanked him and answered with a sincere tone in his voice, "Destiny is bringing us together." They raised the wineglasses again, but *Limón*'s wineglass slipped from his left hand and fell. "It landed on its base," Limón exclaimed. "That's a bad omen sign. Something bad is gonna happen." Pablo calmed him down telling him that death is not written, and he spread again the phrase that always accompanied him, "*No one dies on the eve.*"

That night, he was quiet. He read my card, in which I expressed to him all my love, and I encouraged him to go on. He picked up all of our family and friends' letters, and he gave them to Lucila in a paper bag. "*Burn them,*" he said. Meanwhile, he would go out for a ride in the taxi. He visited friends and trustworthy workers, and once the morning started, he met with our mother. "Mother, this is the last time we see each other in Medellin. On Sunday, I'm leaving for a place in the rainforest," he said.

He explained that he had the assemble of a political group ready, which was going to be called *Antioquia Rebelde* (*Rebel Antioquia*), with which he would fight for the liberation of the department. "We will be a country, and I will be the president." Mom approved his idea, and she expressed this with support and encouragement in her voice. She said goodbye with a kiss on his forehead, and she hugged him. "I love you, don't forget that," she told him. Mom took him by the arm and accompanied him to the house door, in which they conversed. It was five in the morning on December 2nd.

He finally went to sleep. He woke up at one in the afternoon, and he turned the radio on to listen to the news at that time. He had eggs with fried banana for breakfast. He read the newspaper, and he got up. In the hall, he leaned through the window, and he saw that everything was very quiet. The sky was cloudy, and it threatened to rain. He felt cold. He told my cousin to pass him a blue sweater from the wardrobe, and he put it on. He used the same blue jean trousers as the day before. He didn't want to wear the white tennis shoes. He walked barefoot. Limón was getting the mail bag ready. Pablo talked very little. He told the cousin to take a taxi to the center of the city to do some shopping for him.

"You know where the place is. Buy me some German scissors," he indicated to Lucila. Pablo referred to a store in San Ignacio Park, exclusively for medical supplies, the only place where he could find good scissors for cutting his beard. "I will trim up my beard today," he said.

He also asked her for Christmas cards, a block to write letters, pens, toothpaste and a Gillette shaver. He reminded her to do the entire trip to the store in one hour and a half. As usual, as he had already told her, if she didn't come back in that timeframe, he had to move to another house. Lucila left for the store.

Outside, a taxi had stopped for her. Next to her, a woman about 60 years old was also waiting for a taxi. Suddenly, the woman fainted. My cousin preferred to stay a little bit longer with her and helped her to get into the taxi that she had just stopped. Lucila then waited for another taxi. Ten minutes later, an old car passed by, and she took it. She bought everything on the list, and came back towards the house. It took her one hour and fifty minutes. She got off two blocks before the house and walked. When she arrived at the corner, she bumped into a cop who was running in the opposite direction with a weapon in his hand. She got scared. She continued on her way to the house, and she stopped walking when she found more uniformed cops, who were running from side to side. Suddenly, there was confusion. She got closer to a scared young agent who was waiting beside a tree. "What happened, officer?" she asked. "We have Pablo Escobar, we've shot him down." My cousin dropped the package, and she felt the world spinning around her. Her legs shook, and she smelled death. She didn't have the strength to go on. She sat on the platform and cried. "Why, he was a good man?" she screamed. The agent got closer to her and asked her if she knew Pablo, and she didn't want to answer. She ran away from there, and never went back.

They had located him because of a call he made from the mobile phone that I had sent to him through *Limón*. When the Search Block arrived, Pablo was talking to Juan Pablo, and giving him instructions for an interview for the *Semana* magazine (*Week*). He was dictating the answers that were supposed to appear in the questionnaire that Juan Pablo had in his possession. A device used by the DEA had located Pablo's voice. The phone had killed him. Pablo, who so many times had forbidden us to use the phone for our own safety. He, who always said that there were only four ways to die, "Your girlfriend, your mother, the person that betrays you, and the phone."

At the same time, in the jail, I was receiving the book that Pablo had sent to me. I opened it, without knowing what was going on, and I read, "For my soul brother. My best friend. For him to learn a little bit more about sports, and someday be able to beat me." He signed VP. I didn't understand the signature, because he always signed as Doctor Salustiano or Echavarria in the letters that he sent to me. When the letters were really secretive he signed as *Teresita*, honoring the housekeeper who accompanied us when we were newborns. But I never knew what *V.P.* meant. It may be the only secret that he never revealed to me. Today, sitting here on the side of my bed, I'm still trying to figure out what he meant.

My mother and my sister Gloria arrived at the house where Pablo was killed. First, they found *Limón* lying on the ground in the street. My mother recovered a glimmer of hope when she saw him because she thought that they had mistaken *Limón* for Pablo, and that Pablo was still alive. An official got closer to her and told her, "Your son is the one who's up there, on top of the house," he indicated. My mother discovered him laying over the clay tiles of the roof. They let her up through the staircase in the home, and then she saw him. He had the German Sig Sauer gun in his hand, and then she saw the bullet hole in his head. It was then that my mother remembered his secret deal that he once revealed during the escape from the estate of *El Loro:*

ESCOBAR, INC.

Me and Pablo had first started Escobar Inc a day after the assassination of the Colombian Minister of Justice Rodrigo Lara Bonilla. Pablo was worried about possible retaliation, so we used the company to conduct international business. Before this, we had mainly just used cash as a means of payments, and there was really no need for any formal company. We had used a few different companies in Panama, to facilitate the ownership of real estate and such things that we owned outside of Colombia, for example in Miami, USA. However, in Colombia it was never needed to have any kind of companies. Nobody dared to even think about asking me and Pablo about ownership or to question any such things, life was much easier.

The company and all of our activities was put on hold when my brother decided to go on the run by himself in 1992, and when I went to prison that same year.

In 2014, I met with a young man by the name of Olof K. Gustafsson and I hired him as my new CEO of Escobar Inc. We re-established and re-incorporated our company together, with headquarters in Puerto Rico, USA and also based here in Medellin, Colombia. The name of our company is Escobar Incorporated and through the company, we own all the rights to license any products bearing the Escobar name and the Pablo Escobar name. I am trusting, wholeheartedly the future legacy of my brother, Pablo, and myself, and my family, the Escobar family, in the hands of my very dear friends of Escobar Inc. I ensure that we only do the high-end deals. The best deals. The deals that Pablo would have loved.

Throughout the years we have successfully won a case against Netflix Inc, where we settled out of court. That case started in July of 2016 and settled in November 2017. Earlier, On September 11, 2017 Carlos Muñoz Portal, a location scout working for Netflix was found assassinated in his car in Mexico. The Press tried to twist it to make it seem I had some involvement in this, and that is just lies and lies by the American Press. I had no involvement, he was a guy that clearly did not care for his life, walking around in Mexico in cartel territory with big cameras. That is like walking into a Zoo full of lions with bloody meat in your hands.

In 2017, a man came to my house from Australia, representing to me that he was working closely with Elon Musk of Tesla Inc. I had presented him with a deal, and the deal was that they were to license my flamethrower design and start manufacturing. So they did a year later, and without paying me. We settled this after, as Elon Musk understood that it was not very smart to not pay me. He tried to evade payment, but of course was unsuccessful.

In late 2019 we won a case against a cybersquatter that had stolen our domain name www.pabloescobar.com. We now control and own it 100%. I have big plans for that website, as an addition to our www.EscobarInc.com domain. We also own many other names such as pabloescobar.co and of course my own name robertoescobar.com.